INSIGHT COUNSELING

A PROBLEM-SOLVING APPROACH

INSIGHT COUNSELING

A PROBLEM-SOLVING APPROACH

GET THE S.P.I.C.E^3
GET THE CLIENT STOKED

GARY R. FORD MBA, PhD

INSIGHT COUNSELING
A PROBLEM-SOLVING APPROACH

Published by Insight Publishers

Address: Thorsby, Alberta, Canada

Website: www.garyrford.ca/insight

Edited, designed and typeset by the Author

Printed in the United States of America or Canada

ISBN: 978-1-7750699-2-8

DEDICATION

Dedicated to counselors who help others to solve problems. I salute you as change agents and thank you for working to be the best counselor you can be.

TABLE OF CONTENTS

PREFACE

I remember the days when I underwent my initial training as a counseling psychologist. At the time, training generally involved instruction in Rogerian counseling. It was generally believed that a counseling student who worked in this way could do little harm.

This counseling approach derived from the writings of Carl Rogers in the 1940s on person-centered therapy and became particularly popular in the late 1950s and early 60s. This approach involved reflecting back what the counselor was getting from the client in order to help the client to better understand him or herself.

Carl Roger's premise was that this deepened understanding would, in and of itself, help clients to bring about personal change. Rogers argued people have an inherent drive to grow and a supportive, understanding counselor could help clients to better understand their needs and to discover their own solutions to their own problems and act on them. By offering empathy and what Rogers called unconditional positive regard (personal respect), the counselor was responsible only for the use of active listening skills to reflect back what the counselor was hearing and seeing from the client.

However, this approach gave the counselor no overall strategic structure to move the client forward. The counselor could only follow along as the client stumbled his or her way through the client's story.

Many clients weren't seeking unspecified personal growth or looking for therapy to fix broken parts of themselves. Many clients were simply looking for counseling to help deal with a present-day problem, a difficulty for which the client was having trouble finding a workable solution.

It's tough for a client to find solutions to his or her own difficulties without any structure for effective problem-solving. This is true particularly if the client's existing problem-solving skills are less than effective.

Over time, I learned I needed to do more than offer a verbal mirror to such clients, more than show empathy, and more than feel unconditional positive regard. I needed to help clients solve their own problems so they could achieve personal change and greater success, plus help them to learn how to do this on their own after the counseling relationship was finished.

I decided to write this book to help those of you who want to be practical problem-solving counselors, social workers, volunteer peer counselors, mentors, life coaches, or personal support providers to others in distress. I intend this book to be an adjunct to any training you receive from your employers or educational institutions; or to be a helpful guidebook for those who aren't getting much in the way of practical training for how to be an effective counselor.

For purposes of readability, these words will be used throughout this book to refer to the parties involved:

- counselor = someone who has been tasked with helping others to solve practical personal problems in a counseling, coaching, mentorship or supportive interaction.

- client = the recipient of counseling, coaching, mentorship, or personal support service, usually an individual dealing with a particular issue or affliction that the individual feels is overwhelming.

- counseling – a process where one person helps another person to better understand his or her problems and to deal with personal or situational issues by problem-solving more effectively.

- counseling session = a meeting that takes place between two people, where one of them is assumed to be the helper whose role it is to help the other person resolve a particular issue.

In this book, when I write the word "counseling", I mean a process with a present and future focus – a focus on clarifying the current problem the client needs assistance with, and finding new solutions that lead the client to positive change. This is about helping your clients solve a present and real problem.

I do **not** mean a process of psychotherapy focused on helping the client to resolve psychological trauma's, unfulfilled needs, or repetitive feelings of despair, loneliness, compulsion, anger, doubt or fear, usually triggered by earlier events in the client's life. There are certainly other therapeutic methods available for such issues, but they are not addressed in this book. If you wish to be a well-rounded counselor, I heartily encourage you to also read and learn about many different therapeutic modalities.

The insight counseling process is about looking forward, looking to achieve successful pragmatic solutions that solve present day problems and improve the client's current situation. In addition, in this approach, the counselor helps the client learn how to be a more effective problem-solver in the future.

Insight counseling is about change and problem-solving – more specifically about helping others to undergo change and solve their own problems. Consequently, I think counselor training should include training in:

- effective skills for achieving full understanding;

- a process that helps another person get ready for change;

- skills to work around client resistance to change;

- skills to help clients engage in effective problem-solving to achieve desired change;

- skills to separate oneself from the client's problem so the weight of that problem isn't transferred to the counselor's shoulders;

and,

- skills to sustain one's own health and vitality while taking on the counseling role.

This book addresses these needs and can be useful to anyone who takes on the counseling, coaching, mentoring or support role.

UNDERSTANDING CHANGE

(AND RESISTANCE TO CHANGE)

Counseling is about facilitating change. Understand how and why people choose to make a significant personal change, understand why they resist that change either deliberately or unconsciously, and use a counseling approach that best fits the change process.

Insight Potential When Helping Clients Change – Help your clients to open their minds to positive change and they will see new opportunities for improvement in everything around them. You will be able to help each client be a more intentional problem-solver. Growth and development will accelerate for your clients and you will increase your chances for greater success.

READINESS FOR CHANGE

The first step in building your skills as a counselor and change agent, is to reflect on how you experience the change process. Reflect on your own experience of dealing with personal problems. Particularly, think about those times when you resisted change – either when you worked hard to restore order when you thought it had collapsed because of outside influences, or when you spent time lamenting what happened to you. Think of those frustrating times when you tried to get back what you lost, to get back to the way things were, instead of embracing the change and looking for new opportunities and outcomes.

As human-beings, we have a natural inclination to resist change. We strive to maintain our status quo. Our status quo is the existing state or condition, the way things are and have been – the everyday way of being to which we are accustomed. In general, we tend to regard change as uncomfortable, even distressing, disruptive, or possibly painful.

However, even when we associate our status quo with comfort and predictability, it isn't without problems. There are frequently reasons for change but we have the ability to ignore them, removing them from our conscious thinking and stuffing them into our subconscious mind.

Conscious = the thoughts, sensations, feelings, memories, and needs of which we are aware. We are using our conscious mind when our mind is aware of what it's thinking, experiencing, and doing.

Subconscious = occurring below conscious awareness. The subconscious part of our brain performs without our having to consciously think about it. It stores memories, knowledge, skills and feelings that aren't currently in our awareness (sometimes referred to as unconscious operation within our brain). It also manages the involuntary processes of our body such as breathing, and directs our conscious attention to threats or desires. The subconscious is a source of creative thinking most notably while we sleep, dream, fantasize, or meditate – those times when conscious thinking doesn't interfere.

With our symptoms, problems, discomforts, and even pain stuffed into our subconscious, we have the ability to ignore, deny or minimize the need to change. For the most part, through the process of evolution, we've been programmed as human beings to keep things the same, predictable, safe. We can do this even when we aren't so safe, aren't very pleased with how things are, and even when we hurt. We get into a thinking state where we believe that the way of life we know is better than the way of life we don't know.

If you're going to help others, you need to understand how to overcome this natural tendency to resist change, how to help them get ready for change, how to shift them to an eagerness to solve their problems, and how to shift them to welcoming new opportunities and outcomes. You need to understand how to be a change agent.

So let's examine how people get ready for change. Apply these ideas and concepts to your own experience and test their validity against what you know about how you get ready for change.

Readiness For Change

		State	Common Emotions	Intentions
GREEN	**GO** Zone	Ready for Change	Eagerness, Excitement, Expectations,	We know what we can do, so let's do it.
YELLOW	**WAIT** Zone	Accepting Status Quo	Calm, Comfortable, Accepting	Let's just stay the same.
RED	**STOP** Zone	Stuck and Pained	Loss, Frustration, Irritation, Anxiousness	We really need to do something but can't.

Readiness for change is based on three different emotional states. A person can be in a state of high readiness for change (*the green "GO" zone*), or in a state that is simple acceptance of his or her current situation (*the yellow "WAIT" zone*), or in a state where he or she feels stuck and pained in some particular way (*the red "STOP" zone*).

3

Our normal human inclination is to get into and stay in the "WAIT" zone. We generally come to associate this with comfort, satisfaction, and acceptance of what we have. This place is presumed to be stress free and we adapt in little ways to keep it that way. In such an emotional state, we choose not to face and look at the unpleasant, disappointing, or frustrating aspects of our world. Our attitude is "Let's just stay the same."

It's safe to say there are always problems within any given status quo – most are small, but some may be big. However, to maintain a state of comfort (*the "WAIT" zone*), we have the capacity to subconsciously deny either the existence or consequences of the problems. It's as if our brain functions to keep us in a state of equilibrium by denying or covering over any reasons to change. It's as if we unconsciously think to ourselves, "This is just the way things are."

Situation

Problems
(Barely understood, and underappreciated)

**Living With
The Situation.
No Change
Is Likely.**

Problems have symptoms, many of which we ignore. In some cases, we might acknowledge some minor symptoms while ignoring major ones. It's as if the minor symptoms distract us, and we give ourselves permission to think they're acceptable so we have no reason to change.

This ability is so inherent that human beings can accept serious dysfunctional symptoms as just normal. In paying attention to only some of our symptoms, we often fail to interpret what our problems really are. Too often, we think we have one problem when we actually have another.

If we allow awareness of the real problem to surface, it's likely we will downplay the significance of the problem – "Yes, it can be frustrating when that happens, but it's no big deal." To minimize the significance of our problems, we ignore the consequences of those problems, or treat the costs of the problems as inconsequential. By doing so, we minimize our motivation to make any sort of change.

In turn, new opportunities might present themselves, but to pursue them would mean giving up what is predictable, safe, comfortable. We can even ignore the promise of great benefits by focusing on the great risks that would have to be taken and the potential for failure.

If directed to explore the implications of those problems or ignored opportunities, we confront the costs – both tangible and intangible.

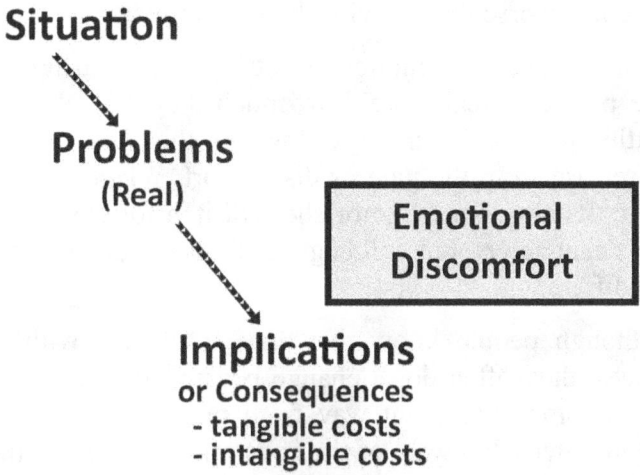

Situation

Problems
(Real)

| Emotional |
| Discomfort |

Implications
or Consequences
- tangible costs
- intangible costs

Tangible Costs	What we currently pay to do what we do. These costs have clear financial measures.
Intangible Costs	Costs that may be more emotional than dollar based, or dollar based costs where it's hard to accurately measure the financial implications. Intangible costs include the negative emotions we live with, the needs that go unsatisfied, the benefits (known and unknown) that we don't get to experience.

If people don't acknowledge and truly experience these tangible and intangible costs, they're likely to prefer the status quo over change.

However, when a person focuses on the implications or consequences of the problems, he or she begins to realize there is an irritation or some form of negative feeling. Realizing how much the status quo actually costs can induce some degree of emotional discomfort, becoming a first level catalyst for change.

This could be experienced as disappointment, irritation, frustration, exasperation, even the more intense emotional pain of loss, regret, and grief; or just simply a state of wanting better results. That acknowledgment of the degree of negative feelings comes as an insight – the problem is worse than previously thought.

Once these negative emotions are triggered by insight as to how serious the problems really are, how much they actually cost, people move a little bit toward wanting change. In this state, we want some degree of release from the pain or discomfort. When the person can't ignore the costs any longer, he or she will itch for change. He or she likely won't change yet, but will begin to think seriously about needing something different.

Even though people know they have problems with significant consequences, they often don't change because they feel constrained, prevented in some significant way from making things better. They become more intensely aware of the constraints that block their ability to make that change.

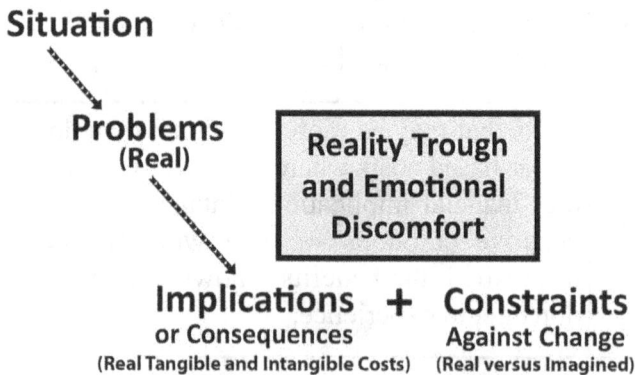

Situation

Problems
(Real)

**Reality Trough
and Emotional
Discomfort**

Implications **+** **Constraints**
or Consequences   Against Change
(Real Tangible and Intangible Costs) (Real versus Imagined)

This results in discouragement, frustration, perhaps hopelessness and despair if the costs are high and the roadblocks are seen as insurmountable (*being in the "STOP" or stuck zone*). I call this the Reality Trough – a conscious awareness of the costs and constraints, and the feelings that accompany that awareness. Once in the Reality Trough, a person realizes the low point of his or her current situation and feels stuck.

People can be in the "STOP" or stuck zone and still not yet have full awareness of the problems and the costs of those problems. This might be quite common amongst those people who use the services of a counselor. Often, they know they're in dire straits but don't really understand their problems, the costs of those problems, and the real need to do something different from what they've been doing to cope. As well, they often believe there are insurmountable constraints in their way.

They will likely complain about the need to change, may look and sound like they want change, but are still in a state of resistance. For real change readiness to emerge, the person must gain true awareness of both the full implications of staying the same and the real constraints that block progress.

Some of these constraints will be real. As such, change is only possible if a solution overcomes or removes the constraint. However, we also tend to imagine constraints. For example, these imaginary roadblocks could be a perceived lack of resources, even though we may have what it will take to make the change. Or the imagined roadblocks could be arbitrary rules we somehow impose on ourselves, even though no one in authority actually put these rules in place. Alternatively, despite evidence to the contrary, we might feel blocked because we have a belief we aren't physically or emotionally capable of effectively making the change.

Once perceived constraints are really explored, people become more aware of which are real and which are imagined. Sometimes, just thinking about their excuses, while facing the real costs of not changing, will cause people to realize the reasons aren't limiting after all. Upon this realization, the imagined constraints can be set aside. Once a person does this, the solution only has to overcome the real constraints.

Instead of denial, the person confronts the reality of his or her own situation and experiences the related emotions. In this state, a person is likely to be on the lookout for how things could be made better. New expectations begin to emerge.

He or she first starts to form minimal expectations as to what change would have to deliver. These minimal expectations seldom reach beyond what he or she already has and seldom involve any significant perceptual shift. In its simplest form, the person may wonder if a small change would accomplish enough gain to be worth undergoing. At this stage, goals are still relatively low.

However, if this person dwells on what he or she would **really** like to achieve and manages to reframe his or her thinking around new higher-order wants and desires, then excitement grows. With new insights about the additional results that the person would really like to accomplish, the person becomes eager for change. A new goal takes shape.

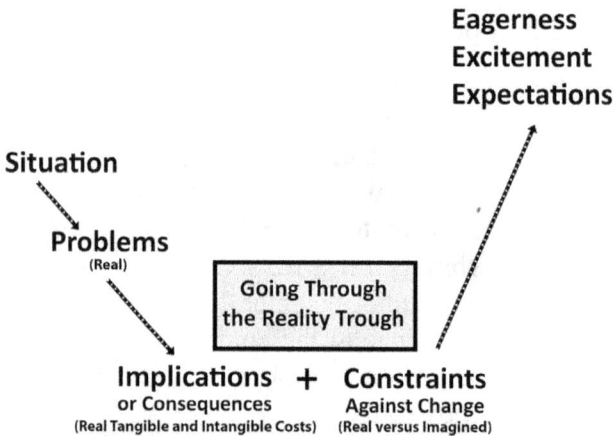

Eagerness
Excitement
Expectations

Situation

Problems
(Real)

Going Through
the Reality Trough

Implications **+** **Constraints**
or Consequences   Against Change
(Real Tangible and Intangible Costs)   (Real versus Imagined)

It's imperative that the much better results appear achievable. Believing the better results aren't achievable, the person may initially hesitate to reframe his or her thinking into a desire for greater outcomes. Alternatively, he or she may even second-guess his or her right to hold such desires.

But if an individual can come to think the higher order goal is achievable, and he or she deserves better, he or she will make a dramatic paradigm shift accompanied by growing excitement. He or she will no longer want to settle for what he or she has. In fact, the person will shift to wanting change now.

From this excitement, the person moves to an eagerness to find a way to make things better as soon as possible. A deadline will emerge in this person's mind along with an impatience to get what he or she wants. At this point, readiness for change has been achieved.

The person in this state is much more likely to go after what he or she really wants. He or she may do this in small ways, like just listening to whatever relevant information comes into his or her world, or in big ways such as initiating a search for a truly valuable solution. Instead of wanting to stay the same, this person really wants to achieve a different and better outcome.

This exploration of the real costs of the problems, the discovery of the real constraints, and consideration of what could ideally be achieved, involves going through the Reality Trough to reach an eager, excited state of readiness for change. I call this insight process, the S.P.I.C.E.^{3} Sequence:

- **S**ituation or status quo,
- **P**roblems,
- **I**mplications of those problems,
- **C**onstraints, and
- **E**xpectations, **E**xcitement and **E**agerness.

When people gain insight as they explore their own S.P.I.C.E.^{3}, they're increasingly ready to undergo change. They have a clear hope things can get better, and a desire to achieve that outcome.

* * *

So as you reflected on how you personally achieved readiness for change at various significant moments in your life, did you see that process in operation? In recognizing that you had to give up the comfort of what you knew for the unknown, did you encounter your own Reality Trough? Did you have to acknowledge how much staying the same (failing to make a change) was actually costing you? Did you examine your own constraints and determine what was real and what was just excuses to keep from making the change? Then did you come to terms with what you really wanted, what would truly excite you enough to want to leave your comfort zone and reach out for something new?

I'll bet you did, but as with most people, much of this might have been below your conscious awareness. To me, this S.P.I.C.E^3 cycle seems to be the normal human path for bringing about voluntary personal change. However, not all change is voluntary.

Involuntary change is something that is forced on us. This usually follows some form of significant catastrophe, and even then, we often fail to thrive in the new circumstances because all of our energy is directed toward getting back what we lost. We focus on returning to the old status quo instead of adapting to the new conditions of life or work.

Many of the clients you counsel will likely be in a state of coping with involuntary change. You can help them take control over their own life and make a voluntary change for the better. You can help them through the S.P.I.C.E^3 sequence to readiness for change. This is a real challenge, but one that is made more manageable when you understand this change process.

When we blend the Readiness to Change model with the S.P.I.C.E^3 Sequence, we can better understand what it takes for people to get ready to change.

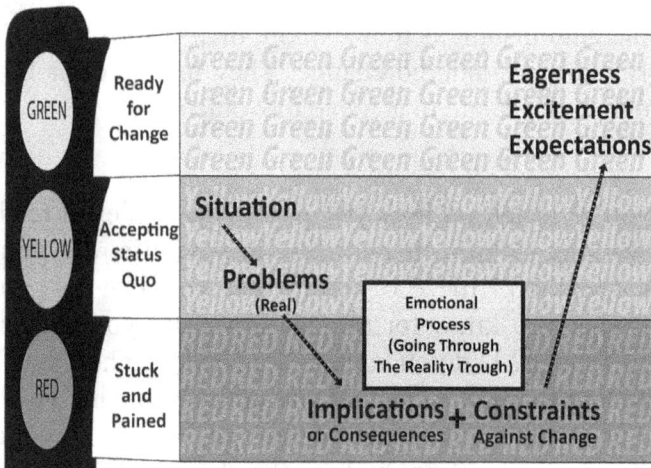

An individual has to move from the comfort of his or her status quo, travel through the Reality Trough to confront the implications of

staying the same, bump up against what he or she believes to be roadblocks, and then consider what could be gained if a change is made. Then healthy change occurs once a person clearly sees the possibility of real solutions to real problems. People change when in the green "GO" zone.

The initial portion of counseling is all about helping a client move into the green "GO" zone. Because of a natural tendency to deny problems and their costs, the counselor must help clients to bring the Reality Trough into full awareness. This is an insight-oriented approach.

As a counselor, you help your client discover urgency to give up the old to acquire something new. Giving up the familiar for something new has tangible costs as well as emotional costs. The person experiencing these costs and emotions must come to believe the new state, and the gain to be had, is worth the price to be paid.

THE COUNSELOR'S ROLE

By asking the right questions and leading the conversation with active listening skills, you steer the client's attention to readiness for change. You want to hear the client go from,

"Things are okay the way they are."

to

"Well, I'm frustrated by... but I can live with it."

through

"I guess the costs are bigger than I thought."

and

"I can't do anything because...."

to

"You mean things really could be better?

to

"Wow! The benefits would be....".

and finally to

"How do I do this?"

Do this with each client to get your clients ready for the second part of the counseling process – finding new solutions that will lead each client to a better way of being.

CLIENT TYPES

In your counseling role, you'll likely encounter clients in different states of readiness for change, and you'll need to feel comfortable exploring the S.P.I.C.E^3 with each of them.

EAGER CLIENTS

Some clients will ask to talk with you. They'll be eager to talk but not necessarily for the purpose of making a personal change. This person might be lonely, feel a compulsion to talk about what has happened to them, or just want to explore what seeing a counselor means. In a few cases, such a person might even be eager to see if there is anything they need to change. You have to be careful when working with such an eager client that you don't get seduced into believing that he or she has a clear and full awareness of his or her own S.P.I.C.E^3.

First off, don't assume this eager client knows he or she has a problem and knows what that problem really is. In turn, the client may not have felt the full extent of the implications of his or her problems and not yet appreciate how bad things really are. This will mean a lower incentive to find an optimum solution.

On the other hand, this client may know exactly what problems he or she is trying to solve, but may not yet fully appreciate what a solution has to deliver in terms of improved results. There may not be sufficient understanding of the potential benefits he or she wants to achieve.

Break free of any assumption that you don't have to take time to learn this eager client's S.P.I.C.E^3. You still need to help this client truly appreciate the full extent of his or her needs. The best assumption is to presume that this client is also resisting change because he or she hasn't yet explored his or her S.P.I.C.E^3. This client needs to fully experience his or her Reality Trough and clarify new expectations and desires.

CURIOUS CLIENTS

Some clients will ask to meet with you just because they want to see what the counseling experience is like, or to see if you're a good person to visit with, or to find out if you're someone who is willing to listen to them tell their story, or to find out if you have a good solution to their problem. This doesn't mean that such clients are motivated to change, or that they even recognize that problems exist within their status quo. Being curious doesn't mean readiness to change. You will need to move this client type through the Reality Trough within his or her S.P.I.C.E.[3] to bring about a shift from being curious to a readiness for change.

DISINTERESTED CLIENTS

Given that clients come to you, you may not expect to encounter disinterested clients, but it's likely you will. Somehow, they find their way into counseling sessions – most typically because someone has told them they should talk with you. Often these clients strongly hold a belief things are okay the way they are.

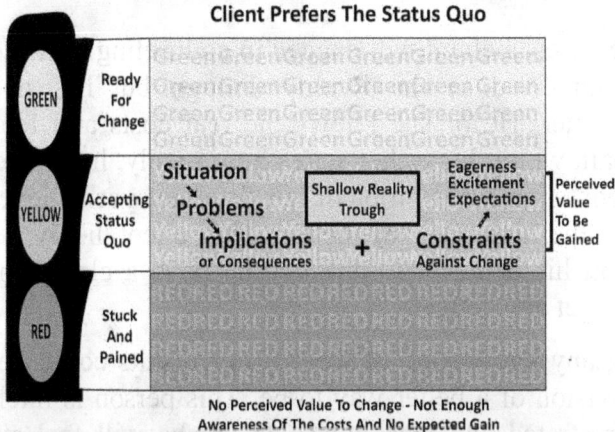

Client Prefers The Status Quo

GREEN	Ready For Change
YELLOW	Accepting Status Quo
RED	Stuck And Pained

Situation → Problems → Implications or Consequences

Shallow Reality Trough

Eagerness Excitement Expectations / Constraints Against Change

Perceived Value To Be Gained

No Perceived Value To Change - Not Enough Awareness Of The Costs And No Expected Gain

This can be the case even when the person complains extensively about the way things are. Some actually use the pain they experience as an excuse to get attention. In this way, they get a reward for what they experience and don't want to give that up.

Alternatively, a person in this state may agree he or she has problems within the status quo, but doesn't consciously experience much pain. If a client doesn't experience any pain or see how to derive any better benefits from change, he or she will prefer to stay the same and not change. Many counselors find these clients hard to work with because the client has no perceived need for making any change.

There's just not enough excitement for change. The value of change is believed to be too small. This client chooses to live by the axiom, "The devil you know." However, below their level of awareness, such clients do have real problems and needs, and could potentially benefit from a counseling experience that helps them to deepen their awareness of their Reality Trough and to find new solutions.

You need to help this disinterested client to fully examine his or her S.P.I.C.E.[3], to uncover the true problems and the real consequences of staying the same, of not changing, of not finding a better solution. You must facilitate insight within the disinterested client and help him or her to develop a heightened awareness of the real costs and degree of actual pain.

DISCOURAGED CLIENTS – WITH LOW HOPE FOR GAIN

In some cases, a client will engage in counseling because he or she is deeply immersed in the Reality Trough but has no hope for something better. He or she knows the real costs and feels the true degree of pain within his or her status quo. Likely, he or she has some thoughts about fixing the problem but does not yet believe he or she could make the situation any better. This client likely sees certain constraints in his or her way and doesn't have a clear sense of how things could get any better.

Lacking any knowledge of what better results could be achieved, there is no vision of a better way to be. This person is likely going to feel very frustrated and lack hope. He or she will feel stuck in the painful "STOP" zone. Out of this pain, this person may want to talk to a counselor only to reiterate his or her story to justify his or her feelings of hopelessness. The attitude conveyed by this discouraged person is likely to be one of "Look at how bad it is - poor me".

The client may be bitchy and angry, and may even direct that at you with a refusal to accept your help. This person wants change badly, but doesn't yet see the possibility of change. In this place, the client is stuck in his or her current way of looking at the world. This client has unconscious blinders on thereby preventing a new perception of the better way things could be.

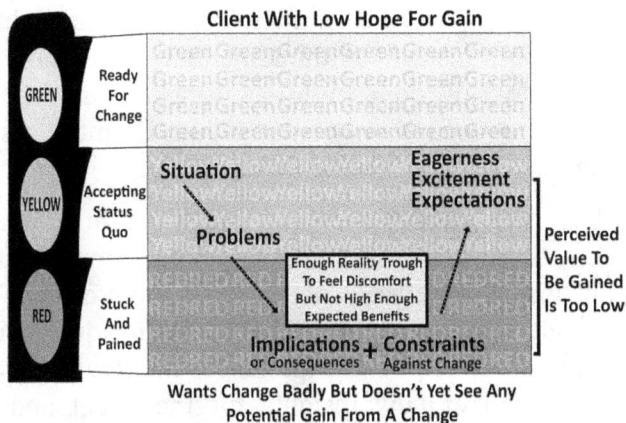

Client With Low Hope For Gain

GREEN — Ready For Change

Situation

Eagerness Excitement Expectations

YELLOW — Accepting Status Quo

Problems

Enough Reality Trough To Feel Discomfort But Not High Enough Expected Benefits

Perceived Value To Be Gained Is Too Low

RED — Stuck And Pained

Implications or Consequences + Constraints Against Change

Wants Change Badly But Doesn't Yet See Any Potential Gain From A Change

As the counselor, lead the client to new ways of thinking about what could be achieved, move past any barriers the client might experience, and raise the client's expectations. Steer the client's attention to wondering what he or she could accomplish if an ideal solution exists. Help this client to reframe his or her hopelessness into a desire for a better outcome.

If you do this, a shift in perception is brought about. Instead of dwelling on what can't be achieved, the client is inspired to consider new results. Instead of hopeless thinking, the client shifts to hopeful aspirations.

As the client imagines what would be gained if he or she could find the right solution, he or she becomes excited about those benefits, and eager to make a change. By elevating the client's expectations, and excitement about potential benefits, the counselor will have a client eagerly anticipating the change process.

RESISTANT CLIENTS

Even though a client arranges an appointment with you to have a counseling session, you shouldn't assume that this person really wants to experience change. He or she "knows the devil he or she is living with" and that feels safer than the unknown that is implied by your wish to help them to experience change. It's safest to assume that most clients will unconsciously want to hold on to what they have. Most clients are resistant clients. As willing as they might appear, they are likely to resist anything you do that implies they should change.

In fact, it's best if you take an approach that resists change more than the client does. Instead of thinking that you're going to bring about change, think of counseling as first helping the client to encounter the fullness of his or her status quo. Be more resistant than the client to any thoughts of making quick change.

Engage this client, answer questions and at the same time, trigger a deeper conversation that allows mutual exploration of the client's S.P.I.C.E.^{3}. The initial objective is not to bring about change but to first achieve full understanding of the client's status quo, with all the feelings that surface as he or she experiences the Reality Trough. This discussion could deliver new insights for the client and lead to a modification of his or her prejudice against change, a shift to a real readiness.

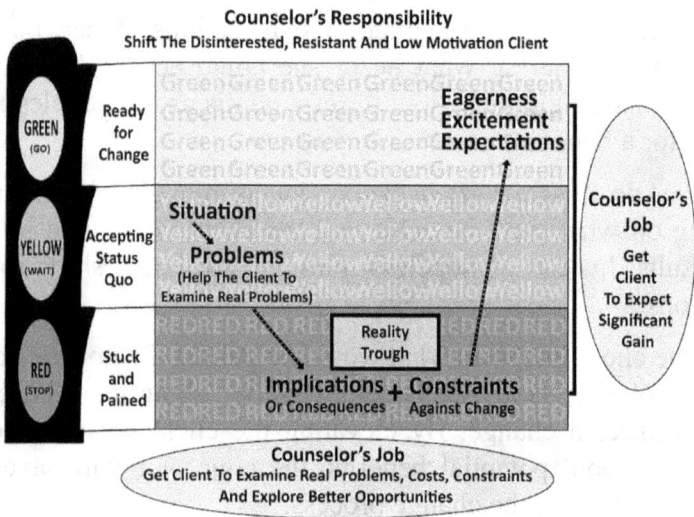

Counselor's Responsibility
Shift The Disinterested, Resistant And Low Motivation Client

To be effective, you need to be able to get into S.P.I.C.E.^{3} conversations with each of these client types. When you do, you will ultimately be counseling with clients who shift to a clear and present desire to achieve a better state of being. You must be the catalyst that shifts each client type to this readiness.

THE REALITY TROUGH

To bring about changes in clients who are prematurely eager to change; those who are just curious, disinterested, or resistant clients; or those with low hope for anything being better than what they currently experience; take the client into and through his or her Reality Trough. As a counselor, you actually have to work to deepen the trough. If a client doesn't experience the emotional discomfort because of his or her denial, you must help the client rise out of denial into a greater awareness of his or her needs.

When discussing the implications of the client's problems, there can be what most people consider to be negative feelings. These feelings are a consequence of expanded awareness and just a natural element of realizing the full costs of the status quo. You should not avoid the surfacing of these feelings. The more intensely the client examines these costs, and the more extensive they are, the higher the client's motivation will be to find a solution.

Looking enthusiastically for solutions will be much more natural when he or she has moved through a deep Reality Trough. He or she will be excited about changing when new insights emerge – insights about the true nature of his or her situation, about the real problems, the full extent of the costs of not making a change, what really stops progress, and what better results could be achieved instead. The client will be ready because he or she now acknowledges the need for a solution, and sooner rather than later.

> At this stage, your goal isn't to get the client to feel better, but to get the client to better feel his or her reality trough.

If you avoid surfacing client feelings, you'll miss opportunities to truly help your clients. Too often, clients have repeated their story to anyone who will listen and have, in the process of repetition, distanced themselves from their underlying emotions. Change won't occur until your client fully understands and feels the implications of his or her problems, and the constraints that block change.

You will be less effective as a counselor if you shy away from your client's expression of his or her feelings. I'm not suggesting your purpose is to induce tears, deep sadness, or pain. Just use the skills known to make it easier for the client to truly explore and experience the consequences of his or her status quo. (See Step Three). If deep feelings are there, let them emerge.

For most problems, the feeling will mostly be surprise as the client realizes what his or her situation actually costs. For some, the realization might be more dramatic as he or she discovers that substantial costs have been ignored.

Be willing to let whatever feelings are there rise to the surface of the client's awareness. Through this insight, the client will be more aware of his or her need to solve the problem and be much more motivated to change.

Later in this book, I address the skills for opening up the conversation so the full extent of the Reality Trough can be discovered and discussed. Using such skills, you will be able to help your clients achieve higher motivation to change. Your clients will want to change and implement the best possible solution for their needs.

THE 12 STEPS TO "GET STOKED & ACT"

> Use a counseling approach that deals effectively with client resistance and best fits with how and why clients become inspired to change.

Insight Potential When Using "GET STOKED & ACT" – *You might find you feel more confident as a counselor because you have a clear purpose, the skills to achieve that purpose, and something satisfying to offer your clients. Your clients will gain insights about their S.P.I.C.E.[3], about effective techniques for creative problem-solving, and about innovative solutions they would likely have never found before your intervention. You might be surprised at the solutions that emerge.*

19

Using the Insight Counseling approach, the initial focus is on a deeper discovery of the client's real and full set of needs. The counselor helps the client to achieve deeper insights about his or her S.P.I.C.E^3, and particularly how the current outcomes experienced by the client fall short of what could be achieved. The counselor's conversation with each client challenges and reframes the client's understanding of his or her own situation, problems, costs, constraints, and opportunities.

The counselor uses the active listening skills of invitations, paraphrases, inference checks, feelings checks, identification, and explained questions to draw out the client's story. But this isn't just a passive approach of following along with the client as he or she tells a story of distress.

In a structured way, the counselor leads the client to share his or her S.P.I.C.E^3. This structure helps the client get ready for change. The counselor challenges the client to think about how he or she would rather be – what better state of being is most desirable to the client, and what potential new results would really motivate the client to make a change.

Insight Counseling involves two main processes – a getting ready for change, and then a search for the right solution that will satisfy the client's needs. The counselor first helps the client to develop new insights about his or her S.P.I.C.E^3, and then helps the client move through an effective problem-solving process to find optimum solutions that could bring about effective personal change.

This insight approach leads to positive change because the client realizes it's better to engage in real problem-solving, consider many possible options, apply a new solution, and achieve previously unanticipated but better results, than it is to do nothing. The client also learns how to subsequently handle future problems on his or her own.

There are various benefits to Insight Counseling. The approach is quite learnable. There is a clear structure and clarity about what skills to use at each step. There is an expectation that the counseling process will lead to client change within a relatively short time frame. Counselors don't just offer unconditional acceptance and provide empathy. They challenge their clients to better understand themselves, to take responsibility for how they're dealing with their own problems, and to pursue a better state of being.

The insight-oriented counselor helps each client to find solutions that offer unexpected new opportunities for the client to succeed. In turn, clients learn to be more self-sufficient problem-solvers following the coaching provided by the counselor.

To help you keep track of where you are in the change process, we use the acronym "GET STOKED & ACT" for the twelve steps in this insight-oriented approach. There are three portions to the counseling process. Part one is dedicated to getting to know your client's problem(s). This initial series of steps involves building rapport with your client, showing empathy and respect, and surfacing a structured understanding of the client's S.P.I.C.E^3.

	STEP	ACTIVITY
G	Greet	Greet the client by showing interest in the client and begin a conversation.
E	Engage	Continue engagement in conversation allowing relationship building to occur.
T	Take Time To Get The S.P.I.C.E^3	Get the client's S.P.I.C.E^3 during an open discussion as you explore his or her needs, taking time to actively listen to the client such that he or she does most of the talking while you clarify for understanding (*reaching for deeper insight*).

After finishing Part One, you make a shift to get into the second portion of the counseling process.

	The Shift	*Once you believe both of you have achieved full understanding of the client's S.P.I.C.E^3, make a mental shift toward inviting your client to engage in problem-solving.*

Part Two is about problem-solving. First, you spend time teaching your client about an effective problem-solving process, and then you guide your client through the appropriate steps. Your task is to stimulate your client's creative thinking and manage your client's critical thinking processes so that an optimum solution emerges.

S	Summarize The Client's S.P.I.C.E^3	Show full understanding by summarizing what you've learned about the client's problem (his or her S.P.I.C.E^3). Present this as the definition of the client's problem, then ask if you fully understand and if he or she agrees that this is the problem that needs to be solved.
T	Teach The Problem-Solving Steps.	Explain that your job is to help your client to solve his or her own problem(s), and then present the problem-solving steps that you're going to help the client to navigate.
O	Option Search (Generate Solution Possibilities)	Engage in brainstorming with your client, provoking your client to participate in creative thinking by using the techniques that stimulate creativity.
K	Know Each Idea Fully (Elaborate And Expand)	Help your client to clarify each of the ideas, add to each idea, and bring ideas together into more complete solution possibilities. Elaborate and expand the ideas into workable solutions.
E	Evaluate	Invite your client to consider the pros and cons of each idea and challenge each idea against the decision criteria contained within the client's S.P.I.C.E^3.
D	Decide (Make The Selection)	Invite your client to choose what he or she considers to be the most optimum solution or set of solutions that will achieve the desired E^3 benefits.

Even though the client has decided what he or she is going to do in order to solve this problem, the process of change is not yet over. You have to help the client to ACT. Part Three is about getting ready to take action and then bringing about the change.

A	Action Plan	Help the client sort out when and where he or she will implement the solution, how he or she will do so, what resources he or she will use, and how the client will keep him or her self on track. Remind the client why he or she is taking each action.
C	Change	If possible, watch or monitor the client as he or she implements the solution to achieve the planned for change.
T	Tally The Results – Assess How Well Both You And The Client Have Done	After the client has implemented his or her solution(s), sit down together and assess how well the solution(s) worked; and talk about how the client feels about the process of change he or she went through. Sort out what the client learned about problem-solving. Sort out what you can learn about being a more effective counselor with your next client.

Using the Insight Counseling approach, you derive confidence from knowing what you're doing. Although you adapt your own behavior in response to each client, you also have an organized agenda you can use to move through the counseling process. This agenda allows you to be comfortable in your own skin when meeting with troubled people.

This agenda adds structure to your counseling process, but it's not carved in stone. I advise you to begin each counselor-client relationship with an intent to work through the twelve steps in order. In some cases, you will complete Part One and recognize a need for therapy to address and resolve old issues, then shift to use of a different therapeutic modality. Alternatively and frequently, you will discover your client just needs to solve a present-day problem, and then you can shift into Part Two of the Insight Counseling approach.

I acknowledge that the abilities of your client will determine the degree of sophistication of the problem-solving skills you will be able to get him or her to use. You need to use this structure while adapting to the abilities and willingness of your client.

Each of the counseling steps calls for specific skills addressed in subsequent chapters. Learn the skills that facilitate effective insight-oriented counseling. Achieving client success will get easier as you gain skill, and as your clients achieve a new proficiency to solve their own problems.

> **Adage:** Give a man an answer to his problem, and he'll have something to resist. Help a man to find his own solutions, and he'll have new ways to solve even more problems, and the excitement to put his solutions into action.

Your clients have needs – problems they would like to solve. You can be the catalyst that helps them address these problems and bring about positive change. You can use the Insight Counseling approach to be a more successful change agent and to help your clients achieve more success in their own situations.

So let's dig into the steps and skills. Get out your yellow marker and make these ideas your own.

PART ONE: THE "GET"

This is the "**GET**" for both of you. Your first task is to get to know the real needs of your client. At least a third of your counseling time should be spent on this first task, and often, you'll spend half your time on the "**GET**". Build an open relationship and encourage your client to share his or her S.P.I.C.E^3 with you, so both your awareness and the client's awareness of his or her full set of needs is expanded. Help the client to get ready for change.

STEP ONE – GREET YOUR CLIENT

You can't be an effective counselor without starting an effective interaction and getting into open and deep conversations with your clients about their needs. You need effective ways to start counseling conversations.

Insight Potential When Greeting Your Clients – *You will gain first impressions of your client, which may give you some immediate clues as to his or her resistance to change, and his or her underlying emotional state. You might learn you need to adapt how you greet in order to meet each particular client in his or her moment. The client might realize he or she really does want to talk with you.*

In your counseling role, approach and greet your clients in a manner they experience as comfortable and supportive. You want your clients to feel a willingness to converse with you. Show each client he or she is valued and respected. Begin with the intention of building an open and constructive relationship. Forming that relationship starts as soon as you and your client meet.

THE GOALS OF THE GREETING STEP

In the Insight Counseling approach, you're a change agent and facilitator of effective problem-solving. If a client has agreed to meet with you, it's safe to assume he or she has a problem to be solved, even if he or she can't yet articulate what that problem really is, or even if denial masks existence of the real problem.

You need to start a relationship in which the client is comfortable enough with you to talk about these problems. Your primary goals at this stage are to:

- create a positive first impression,

- form your own first impressions of the client so you can expand your own understanding of what it feels like for the client to come and talk with you,

- help the client to feel comfortable and welcome,

- establish your credibility as someone that can help,

- begin a conversation where you learn about the client's needs,

and

- help your client develop a willingness to better understand his or her needs.

The ultimate goal of this step is to begin an open and personal conversation.

FIRST IMPRESSIONS

First impressions have a significant impact. You want yours to clearly show each client you're someone who has value to offer. Be seen as someone who your client can trust. Present and act as someone that respects the client and wants to learn more about him or her.

Your own first impression on the client is influenced by many things, some of which are:

- how you dress and your personal grooming,

- your underlying attitudes,

- your demeanor and how you carry yourself (*which is heavily influenced by your attitudes*),

- the expectations you have about the client's possible reaction to you,

and

- your initial greeting behavior (*what you say and what you do*).

You want this first impression to show your client that you're comfortable to talk with and that you have credibility as a change agent.

Consider your personal appearance, your hygiene, your tone of voice, and your body language. Is it appealing enough, fresh enough, comfortable enough, that you're able to get people engaged? Or does it turn people off and create immediate resistance that will take additional time to overcome?

To cause a positive first impression, your interaction with the client requires:

- a comfortable meeting environment free of anything that might stir a negative emotional reaction within the client,

- a warm and sincere smile,

- good eye contact, especially when the client talks to you,

- a non-threatening position relative to the client's personal space,

- a firm but gentle, and humbly offered handshake if circumstances seem appropriate,

- a sincere, enthusiastic, and "welcoming" attitude,

plus

- a warm, respectful, attentive expression of interest in working with the client.

There has to be a connection and you must do everything you can to connect. As you reflect on this very critical step of the counseling process, is there anything about your own first impression that may be getting in the way of your counseling success?

YOUR MEETING ENVIRONMENT

As much as your circumstances allow, be careful about your meeting space. Make sure the client has a comfortable place to sit, and the client is not positioned in any way that means the client is less respected than you are. For example, the client's seat height should be the same as your own. If the client is forced to sit lower than you, this creates a dominant/inferior relationship, which will add to the client's resistance.

The comfort afforded by the client's seating should be no less than your own. Take the least comfortable seating if you have to. The lighting on the client's face should not be any more intense than it is on your own. For example, if your client is forced to sit facing a window, and you have your back to the window, then the client is at a visual disadvantage. Shift so the client isn't forced to look at you as a silhouette, unable to discern your facial features and gestures.

Pay attention to any objects, pictures, or posters in the room that could distract or otherwise trigger a resistant reaction within the client. Anything that might seem derogatory in any way should be removed. If there is anything visible that says or implies, "I'm going to change you." then get rid of it. Be aware of any potentially negative messages conveyed by the objects and furniture in your meeting space.

One counselor I consulted with found he was having difficulty getting his clients to open up. On visiting his office, I found a statue on his desk of a frog that had shot its tongue way out of its mouth to catch a fly and was subsequently unable to reel it back in. This statue directly faced his clients and eloquently communicated, "If you open your mouth around here, you'll just regret it." He had other issues to work on but the first step was to remove this statue from his office.

Dress And Grooming

Dress comfortably, likely in casual business attire. You want to look credible. Dressing in T-shirts, shorts, or wearing shoes without socks is likely too casual. Wearing a full suit and tie or formal business attire is equally inappropriate. Dress with care and for comfort.

Cleanliness and grooming also say a lot about you. Present yourself as a person who cares about him or herself – clean, well groomed, and ready for a personal encounter. If you want to be a successful counselor, pay attention to the details your client will see when he or she first encounters you.

Underlying Attitudes And Your Personal Demeanor

Think of every client as someone who you will eventually help to make an effective change, but first see it as your priority to get to know your client as he or she is right now. In other words, change is not your opening priority. For each client, hold the attitude this person is worth knowing first. Do not approach feeling any pressure to get your client to make a quick change, to suddenly be over the problems that brought the client to you. There should be no pressure to bring about change because you know your first priority is to get to know your client.

Believe that your success depends on helping each client to find his or her own success. Assume your task is to help your client achieve better results. Know you can only do this by establishing rapport and winning some trust.

Honor the client's resilience and feel some appreciation for what he or she may have overcome or had to deal with in the past. Look for the client's abilities, drive to survive, positive attitudes, and personal strengths. Treat the client's willingness to visit with you as a sign of bravery, commitment, and desire to achieve something better. See the client as the 'boss of him or herself" and assume you're there to serve the client.

Have a personal demeanor of confidence, mixed with humility and compassion for your fellow beings. This confidence should not come across as arrogance or pretense. Be seen as caring about the client because you do.

Your demeanor comes from your beliefs and attitudes, your goals and motivations. To be effective using the Insight Counseling approach, hold beliefs, attitudes, goals and motivations that favor the client's long term success.

Believe your job is to help your clients to better understand their needs and strengths, and to help them get ready to make changes they want to make for their own well-being. Believe your clients can learn to solve their own problems more effectively and achieve better results. See it as your responsibility to make that learning possible.

YOUR EXPECTATIONS

The expectations you have about a client's possible reaction to your greeting will also show. If you worry about how the client might react to you, your discomfort will transfer to the client and generate some awkwardness for both of you.

The best strategy is to greet without any expectation as to how the client will react to your greeting. Have an open mind, assume anything is possible, and give the client the chance to react in his or her own way. Watch, listen, and feel the client's reaction. Your next response would vary with every person you engage because each relationship is unique.

YOUR INITIAL GREETING BEHAVIOR

What you say and what you do can make a difference. The counselor who steps close to the client with a large smile on his or her face and reaches into the client's personal space to offer a hearty handshake, may come across as TOO friendly. For some clients, this type of assault may be unwelcome. On the other hand, if you are inherently shy and avoid contact because you fear rejection, this will show as a slight hesitation when you greet. Equally awkward is the counselor that stands too far back, fails to make eye contact, and speaks mechanically saying something like, "How can I help you?". The counselor needs to be seen as actually interested, and needs to show that interest.

Pay attention to the behavior of your client and match your greeting to your client. Be warm, welcoming, and as assertive as your client appears to be. The greeting in the insight-oriented approach, should be gentle, respectful, sensitive to the needs of the client, and empathic.

YOUR FIRST IMPRESSIONS OF YOUR CLIENT

In this greeting step, you need to be alert to how your client presents him or herself, and be aware of the first assumptions you make about the client based on that presentation. We innately form first assumptions based on what we see, hear, sense, and what we don't see, hear, or sense as we first encounter another being. As well, we notice when something expected for the situational context does not occur and make guesses about what this means.

These assumptions can be correct or incorrect. If correct, they are important clues about this other person and his or her S.P.I.C.E[3], his or her awareness of that S.P.I.C.E[3], his or her readiness for change, and his or her degree of resistance to change. In addition, you may see clues that give you information about how the client is reacting to you as the designated change agent.

The client knows that coming to talk with you is about change and that can be both exciting and scary. You want to see how the client is reacting to that basic ingredient of this first meeting. Is the client hesitant, withdrawn, shy, closed up in posture, withholding information about him or herself, looking away from you, looking at you cautiously and with suspicion, or apparently angry about having to meet with you? These behaviors likely convey resistance.

Remember, I said earlier you will perform better in bringing about client change if you're more resistant than your clients. By noticing these behaviors, you can be particularly sensitive to your client's need to protect him or her self from you. What you do and say should respect that concern.

The client's behavior will give you initial clues about whether this is an eager, curious, discouraged, dis-interested, or expressly resistant client and you will need to adapt your behavior accordingly. You want to match the client's eagerness and curiosity with your own, just as you want to step gently and carefully when your client is discouraged and down. Show empathy by modifying your behavior to be similar to the client's own behavior.

If the client is showing disinterest or resistance, then adapt and show some of your own resistance to meeting. For example, you could say you sense his or her discomfort about having to meet, you aren't sure that the meeting is appropriate for him or her, and you respect any reservations this client might have about talking to you. In the face of the client's resistance, be careful to curb your own enthusiasm about your desire and ability to be helpful. Move slowly and carefully toward opening up a conversation with these clients.

GREETING

In general, you want to offer a simple greeting that conveys your respect for your client and your appreciation that he or she has come to talk with you. You want to show the client is welcome to your space, you're glad he or she has come, you look forward to the pending conversation, and if you sense hesitation or resistance on your first impression, that you can respect any concerns the client might have about coming to visit with you.

THE FRIENDLY SOCIAL GREETING

Sometimes, the best approach is the friendly, social approach simply saying,

"Hi. How are you doing today?"

or

"I'm glad you've come. I hope you found your way here without any difficulties?"

or

"Great, you've made it. I was just going to get a coffee. Can I get you anything to drink or snack on while we meet?"

Or the counselor could notice something unique about the person, and use this to start a conversation.

"I notice you're wearing a Colts team jacket. I have an interest in the team, and I'm curious about your involvement?"

or

"I see you're wearing a blood donors badge. My brother was just in an accident and needed blood, so thank you for your contribution. Is this something you do regularly?"

If you think about it, this is how you meet people in social circumstances, so use these natural skills to start this conversation.

SIMPLE WELCOME

Another option is to begin with a specific statement of welcome. Give the other person what people normally expect when they first meet each other in a business-like context. Say something like,

"Welcome to (the name of your agency, organization or group)! My name is (*your name*), and I'm glad to meet you. Please take a seat (*while pointing to a comfortable chair*)."

or

"Hello (*client's name*). My name is (*your name while offering your hand for a handshake*). Please join me over here in this comfortable sitting area. I'm pleased to meet you and welcome this opportunity to talk."

SIMPLE WELCOME WITH EMPATHY

If you recognize the client has some hesitation about meeting with you, you could say something like the following to show your empathy and compassion,

"Hello, my name is (*your name*) and I'm pleased to meet you. However, I sense some hesitation on your part, perhaps unsure what it means to visit with me, perhaps even questioning in your own mind why you're here. Am I correct?"

or

"Hello, my name is (*your name*) and I'm pleased to meet you. I know that visiting with a counselor to talk about your personal situation can sometimes be tough. I respect any concerns you might have about this visit. Can we talk about them first?"

If you sense outright resistance to meeting with you, match the intensity of that resistance. If the person conveys anger and resentment toward you, respond with something like,

"My name is (*your name*) and I want to welcome you to this visit. I appreciate you agreed to meet with me but I sense you just don't want to be here, and feel somewhat forced to talk with me. I respect that. I wouldn't want to talk with a stranger about my personal business if I didn't make that choice on my own. I don't intend to make you do anything you don't want to do. Any suggestions for how we could make this seem like a safer place to be."

or

"(*Your client's name*), I'm (*your name*) and I'm here to meet with you to provide assistance as you deal with your (*whatever the client is dealing with*). I notice the grimace on your face and you seem to be fairly tense at the moment. In fact, it seems to me you feel angry and upset about being here. I'm guessing you either don't want to talk with a counselor about what's happening to you, or you've heard something about me that makes you concerned about this session. Is either of these possibilities correct?"

If the person just seems closed and watchful, but isn't conveying anger or resentment, you could possibly say something like:

"(*Your client's name*), please come in and take a seat. I'm (*your name*) and I'm pleased to meet with you. This is our first meeting and I appreciate we don't know how to be with each other just yet. I'm guessing you aren't sure what to expect out of our meeting, and you're worried about what's going to happen during your visit. My expectation is that it's my job to help you feel comfortable here and welcome. Any suggestions for how I could do that?"

Simple Welcome With Declaration Of Purpose

With this type of greeting, you quickly declare your purpose for meeting. You offer a simple greeting then add why you believe the two of you are meeting.

"I'm pleased to meet you. I'm (*your name*), one of the peer counselors here at (*the name of your agency, organization or group*). Like you, I've experienced (*whatever the calamity is that you share with the client*) and I'm here to talk with you about your concerns as you deal with it yourself."

or

"(*Your client's name*), my name is (*your name*) and I'm one of the counselors here at (*name of your agency*). It's my job to provide you with any assistance you might want to better cope with (*the typical issue that brings people to your agency*).

or

"Good afternoon (*your client's name*). I'm (*your name*), one of the counselors here. I want to spend time with you, listen to what you're dealing with, help you to sort out your priorities and figure out what you can do to better deal with your situation."

Simple Welcome With Disclosure Of Your Credentials

There might be counseling situations where your clients will wonder what makes you qualified to be their counselor. You'll need to make a clear disclosure about both your related expertise and limitations. Take the lead in a greeting of this nature – make a simple welcome statement along with a statement about what qualifies you to be a counselor.

"Welcome. My name is (*your name*). I've been assigned to be your volunteer counselor here at (*name of your agency, organization, or group*). I imagine you have questions about me and what qualifies me to be your counselor, so I'd like to start by telling you a bit about myself. I had (*whatever the personal experience is that you had to deal with that the client might relate to*) and I wound up seeing a counselor myself to find better ways to deal with that experience. It was helpful to me and I decided to give back by volunteering to do the same for others. They provided very specific training in how to effectively support others going through what I did. I did well in that training so they gave me this opportunity to be a counselor. I've been doing this for two years now and it's been a very rewarding experience. My performance gets reviewed regularly by my supervisor and my clients rate how helpful I am. According to them, I've done well. I'm hoping I can do the same for you."

or

Welcome to (*name of your agency, organization, or group*). My name is (*your name*) and I've been assigned to be your counselor. I'd like to tell you a bit about myself before we begin. I received my counseling training at (*the name of the educational institution where you undertook your training*) and I've been working in the counseling field for 3 years. I also need to be clear that I haven't personally experienced what you've experienced with (*the nature of the calamity that the client has experienced*). However, I work hard to understand what my clients are going through and help them solve the problems they deal with. Do you have any questions about my ability to be helpful?"

or

Welcome to (*name of your agency, organization, or group*). Please make yourself comfortable (*pointing at a designated chair*). My name is (*your name*) and I've been assigned to be your counselor. I need to be clear upfront that I'm a volunteer. I was trained by (*name of your agency, organization, or group*) to be helpful to our clients. I also need to be clear that I haven't experienced what you've experienced with (*the nature of the calamity that the client has experienced*). I don't pretend to be an expert in what you've had to deal with.

However, I know how to listen, how to understand, and how to help my clients engage in problem-solving to find ways to achieve better results than they currently experience. Do you have any questions about my ability to be helpful?"

or more simply,

"Hello Bill. My name is (*your name*). I'm a certified counselor here at (*name of your agency, organization or group*). Do you have any questions or concerns about me or my credentials as a counselor?"

THE "I HAVE SOMETHING FOR YOU" GREETING

If you're uncomfortable with the other approaches, another option is to begin by offering the client a small gift to start the relationship off. Give something of value, and get into a conversation. You could say something like,

"My name is (*your name*). Our agency offers many different services. Peer counseling is one of them. Here's a brochure for you that lists each of our services. In this section, it explains how our counseling works. Was there anything in particular you were wondering about what we do that I could address?"

or

"Hello Fred. My Name is (*your name*). We have a booklet of community resources that our clients find helpful as they cope with (*whatever the client is known to be dealing with*). I wanted to make sure you have one. (*As he or she reaches out to take it from you*) What led you to ask for this visit today?"

* * *

Find your own way to greet your clients. The key ingredient is to be flexible and use an approach that matches how the client appears as you first meet. The second concern is to use a greeting you feel comfortable using. Your comfort will radiate to your client and make your first connection easier.

Whenever possible, use humor, and playfulness. Get your client smiling, chuckling, laughing with you, and continue the conversation.

When we meet people in social situations, there is often an element of play or having fun. As long as the context in which you do your counseling is not somber, grave and dire, don't be afraid to use humor to make first contact with a client. Get this other person smiling and into a conversation with you.

WHEN TO MOVE TO THE NEXT STEP

Recognize the right time to shift from Step One where you make first contact into Step Two where you get conversational. You know it's time to transition when:

- the client smiles at you,

- he or she maintains eye contact with you,

- you feel like you've initiated some small degree of rapport with the client,

- the client makes a conversational reply,

or

- the client begins to share information about his or her needs.

It should take only a few seconds from the point at which you initiate your greeting to the transition to Step Two where you more fully engage in conversation.

THE TRANSITION TO ENGAGING

Your Greeting will ideally take you to engaging in conversation. There are several ways to transition to the next step:

1. Engage in whatever social chit-chat the client offers up.

   "Yes, the television broadcast of the Royal Wedding was very impressive last night. I gather you were also able to watch it?"

2. Share something of yourself that might be of interest to the client. For example, you might mention something about your own history and similar experiences.

"Just to let you know something about myself. I had (*whatever the similar experience is*) and certainly struggled to cope with what happened. With some help, I found my own way and I'm in pretty good shape right now. In order to give back some of the support I received, I decided to become a volunteer counselor. I'm hoping I can be of assistance to you. "

or

"I've just completed my training as a counselor and have been working at (*name of your agency, organization, or group*) for several months. I'm really enjoying the work and I love meeting with my clients. They've been dealing with some incredible challenges and I've really noticed their resilience and personal strengths. Please tell me something about your own situation?"

or

"Early in my life, I went to university to study geology but got married before I worked in the field. I'm a single parent with two teenage children and I wanted to do something meaningful outside of the house so I volunteered to work with (*name of your agency, organization, or group*). Please tell me something about yourself?"

3. Paraphrase whatever response he or she gives to your greeting.

"Sounds like you had some difficulty finding this place?"

or

"You want to know how this counseling stuff works, is that correct ?"

or

"If I understand correctly, you're just checking me out to see if this could be of any use to you?"

or

"You want to know how to get support services through (*name of your agency, organization, or group*), correct?"

4. Answer any questions the client asks you. Be helpful and positively responsive. Be enthusiastic.

"Yes I'm just a volunteer. I was able to get this opportunity because I too had (*what ever the similar experience is*), dealt reasonably well with what happened, and then took training in how to be helpful to others with a similar experience. Is there anything else you'd like to know?"

or

"Yes, the typical counseling session is about an hour long. If it turns out we need more time, we can schedule another meeting. Does that work for your schedule today?

or

5. Ask your own transitional question to move the focus on to the client's personal experience.

"So what brings you to (*the name of your agency, organization, or group*) today?"

or

"How can I be of assistance?"

or

"I'm guessing you hope to talk with someone that understands what you're going through, and you're wondering if I'm able to do that?"

or

"Do you have any questions about what a counseling session like this involves?"

or

"What got you to make the effort to come to see me today?"

How you transition will depend entirely on how the client responded to your greeting. If he or she began with small talk, then reply accordingly, and then transition to further engagement. If the client asks you a question, then answer that question and transition with something that gets the client telling you about him or herself. If the client makes some sort of declaration, then reply in support of whatever he or she has asserted, and ask for more information about his or her thoughts.

I call this "meeting the client in his or her moment". Socialize if that is what he or she offers; answer any questions; or use a transitional question to remind the client he or she had a purpose, something that motivated him or her to meet with you. You initiate the hello, then attend to the client's response so you can determine how best to keep him or her talking.

How the client responds gives you the information you need to determine what your transition response could be. This requires both your confidence that you can engage this other person in conversation meaningful to him or her, and your flexibility to respond according to what you have been offered by the client.

STEP TWO – ENGAGE

It's not enough to simply introduce yourself to the client. Cause an open conversation to occur and a counseling relationship to begin.

Insight Potential When Engaging – *The client may discover you have something to offer that could bring real value to the client. In turn, the client might become more acutely aware of the loneliness he or she feels in dealing with the problem(s) on his or her own. The counselor may discover information about the client that was not previously known.*

To be successful using the "GET STOKED & ACT" counseling approach, truly master the second step for engaging clients in conversation. Engaging will allow you to transition from the greeting to learning about the client's needs.

THE GOALS OF THE ENGAGING STEP

In the Engaging Step, you have three main goals that should guide your behavior with the client:

- get the client into a conversation with you, most typically by talking about what is of interest to the client,

- build trust and rapport with this client so he or she is comfortable talking with you,

and

- set the stage to begin a focus on the client's needs.

In this step, we engage the client in an expanding conversation. First, "meet the client in his or her moment" and then steer the interaction to a conversation about his or her needs.

Some clients need more engagement after the greeting and before you get to the business of learning their needs. Others may be quite willing to discuss their needs, and open up right away. The ultimate goal isn't just conversation but a conversation where you're able to fully learn the client's S.P.I.C.E^3 in the following step.

ENGAGING EFFECTIVELY

You have to be able to engage clients of all types – eager, curious, discouraged, disinterested, and resistant - and get them into a conversation. This transition step is very important to your success, and ultimately your client's success. Get people talking with you, even when at first it appears they don't want to. Establish trust and rapport early in the conversation so the client will open up to you.

Certainly in many cases, this step will occur as soon as you greet the client. The client might leap into sharing his or her reason for wanting counseling, telling you what he or she hopes to get out of the meeting. If this happens, you have material that will allow you to move right into Step Three where you take time to learn your client's

S.P.I.C.E[3]. Join this client in his or her moment and move right into the purpose of your counseling session.

On the other hand, you will encounter some clients where their resistance to the change process is so substantial that they put up barriers to your engagement. The client might try to take charge by:

- asking many questions as soon as you finish your greeting,

- challenging your expertise or ability to understand and provide assistance,

- launching into a lament or complaint, about what has happened to cause the client disruption and pain, in a way that doesn't allow any real exploration,

- holding back information about him or herself, predominantly through silence, closed posture, short answers to any of your questions, and deflection of your questions such that he or she might speak but not really answer what you asked,

or

- talking about anything but him or herself and changing the subject to less than relevant topics.

You're the counselor and must create a safe atmosphere then gain control of the interaction so you both can begin to work on the problem(s) that brought the client to you.

It's your job to meet the client in his or her moment and use what is relevant to the client to get your conversation going. Don't treat all clients the same way. Pay attention to how he or she acts when you greet and adjust your behavior accordingly.

If your client has questions of you, answer the questions, then ask a question of your own. If your client wants to socialize first then briefly engage in social talk. If your client wants to challenge you, then address the challenge with information that allays the client's concerns. Start from what appears to be important to the client and then steer the conversation to a more open discussion of his or her needs.

ENGAGEMENT STRATEGIES

Engage your client in the conversation that he or she wants to have, and then steer the conversation toward disclosure of the client's S.P.I.C.E.[3]. First, go where the client takes the conversation then exercise leadership when you have rapport. This is your responsibility as a counselor. Be able to get into a conversation with anyone.

GETTING PAST THE FOCUS ON YOUR EXPERTISE

Your client may ask you about your qualifications. Deal with the question in a manner that allows you to move into a deeper conversation.

First paraphrase the question to make sure you understand what the client is really asking. Once you know you understand, and your client knows you have empathy for his or her concern, answer the question. Then, re-direct your client's attention to his or her full set of needs by asking questions that deepen insight and understanding of those needs.

> "Sounds like you're wondering what qualifies me to be your counselor, correct? (*Client nods*) I respect your concern. I'm a registered social worker with four years of experience helping those living on the street like you. How about telling me something about yourself – what brought you in today?"

If the client challenges your right to be his or her counselor, either overtly by making a challenging statement, or more subtly by being reserved and closed, then respond with grace, and appreciation for the client's concern.

> "I'm betting you have doubts about my ability to help you, a much older person with significantly more life experience than I could possibly have? If so, I certainly respect your concern. I'm much younger and I just recently completed my training as a counselor. So it's fair to say I'm pretty green and you're truly the expert on yourself and what you're dealing with. However, in my own defense, I want to emphasize that I want to help you gain the best advantage of your own experience, knowledge and abilities. I'm not going to tell you what you should do, but I have the skills to listen, understand and guide our problem-

solving to help you find a new solution you think will really make a positive difference. Do you have any concerns about this?"

or

"If I was in your shoes, assigned to talk with a stranger about personal issues, and knowing this person is just a volunteer, I'd be suspicious and concerned about his or her ability to help. I'd wonder if he or she has enough training to deal with my stuff. I'd wonder if the counselor ever had to personally deal with (*nature of the experience the client is likely dealing with*). If he or she hasn't gone through it, how could this counselor really understand what I'm experiencing? I'm guessing you have these questions right now?"

Don't argue. Answer any question or challenging statement with the information the client needs. Give any information that might be helpful to the client to accept your assistance. Model openness. Show your client it's safe to openly share feelings and personal information.

Answer your client's inquiry, and then respond with a question of your own to encourage the client to consider some element of his or her S.P.I.C.E.[3]. (*Below,* CR *designates Counselor, and* CT *designates Client.*)

CR: Welcome to (*name of your agency, organization or group*). My name is (*your name*). Please have a seat (*pointing at the appropriate chair*). I'm glad you've come today. I'm here to talk with you about your concerns and needs related to (*the problem that your agency typically deals with*). Tell me about your situation.

CT: I'm not sure you can help me.

CR: Sounds like you doubt that I can understand and appreciate what you're going through, what you really need right now. Is this correct?

CT: That's right. How could you possibly help if you've never experienced what I have?

47

CR: You're worried I have no way to be helpful if I haven't also experienced (*what the client has had to deal with*)?

CT: Yeah, how could you know what I need?.

CR: Well, like you, I did experience my own (*what the client has to deal with*) and had to find my way through. However, you're right, your experience is different and I can't know what you need until you share your own thoughts about that. Please help me to understand and tell me what happened to you. (*and so on to get a conversation going.*)

or alternatively, if you haven't experienced the same dilemma:

CR: You're right, I haven't had to go through what you've experienced. I haven't had the same experience but I've had to deal with my own problems and I know that can be very challenging. If you share your experience with me, I will listen carefully and do my best to understand. Please tell me what you're dealing with that brought you to counseling. (*and so on to get a conversation going.*)

Hopefully, this conversation can be continued so the focus shifts from resistance to an exploration of the client's situation.

Instead of either interrogating the client or simply relinquishing control over the counseling process, respond with re-direction and get to a discussion of needs. To effectively re-direct a client's challenge, you can respond to client questions using this process:

- **clarify** the underlying meaning of the question or challenge (*paraphrase*),

- **agree** with the importance of the question or challenge,

- **answer** the question or address the challenge,

- **explain your intention** to understand his or her needs, and

- **ask** a situation or expectation question.

First, clarify to achieve an understanding of the client's underlying meaning. You would do this because people don't always say what they mean. Then, agree with the client's concern and the importance of the question or challenge. For example, if a client says, "You're just a (*volunteer, new trainee, young kid, middle class white, single person without kids, etc.*). How can you be helpful with problems like I have to deal with?", you could say something like,

> "Sounds like you're wondering what skills I have that qualify me to be a counselor? That's an important concern. You don't want to waste your time talking with someone who doesn't have the skills to actually be helpful, correct?"

Answer the real question or challenge that you uncover, which might actually be what the client asked or said, but could also be something he or she wants to know but is too hesitant to ask directly. It's possible the client could have asked a roundabout question or stated an indirect challenge. Following your clarification, give your answer.

> "I think I can be helpful for two reasons. I've experienced some of what you have in my own life; and (*name of your agency, organization or group*) gives all of its counselors special training in how to achieve full understanding of our client's problems, and how to help client's to use creative problem-solving skills to arrive at better outcomes than they currently experience."

or

> "I haven't experienced what you're dealing with and can't be certain I can be helpful until I learn more about what you're dealing with. However (*name of your agency, organization, or group*) has trained me to use specific skills to better understand your situation and needs, and to help you find new ways that will get you better results."

Then explain your intention to understand all of the client's needs.

> "I'd like to know more about you. I'd like to know what you're dealing with because I want to understand your needs, the problem(s) you're dealing with, and what you would prefer to achieve. Once I have that, we can work together to find new solutions for your issues."

49

Finally, ask a question about his or her current situation or about the results he or she expects to get. For example, you could say:

> "It will help if I understand more about what happened to you and how this has affected you?"

or

> "You've come to our agency hoping to improve something in your life. What results would you be looking to achieve?"

You come across as a more impressive insight-oriented counselor when you clarify, agree, answer, explain and then ask. You meet the client right in his or her moment, and then take control of the conversation to lead it into Step Three – Take Time to Learn The S.P.I.C.E³.

CR: "Welcome to Family Services. My name is (*your name*). Please be comfortable (*pointing at the appropriate chair*). How may I be of assistance."

CT: "I'm not sure you can be. You look much too young to have teenage children?"

CR: (*Clarify Meaning Of The Challenge*) I'm guessing you're feeling quite overwhelmed, uncertain how to deal with the issues your kids bring into the house, probably feeling like you don't have much control over them, and worry I'll have nothing useful to offer, correct?"

CT: "Yes. How can someone as young as you know what I'm going through."

CR: (*Agree With Challenge*) "Given how challenging it can be with teenagers in the house, and given that my age shows I couldn't have raised teenagers yet, that's a valid concern.

CT: "Yes. I need someone to tell me what to do to gain control over these kids."

CR: (*Answer The Question*) "I certainly agree that as the parent, you want to have some authority over what happens at home. (*Explain Your Need To Know More*) It would help me to provide assistance and get you useful answers if you could tell me more about your circumstances. (**Ask About The Client's Situation And Problem**) Please tell me what's going on at home?"

CT: "Well it started about three weeks ago...?

TOUGH CLIENTS

Many counselors say, "It isn't that easy. Some clients are really tough." Well such counselors are right – some clients are a real challenge. It can be a struggle to get conversational with:

- gruff and belligerent individuals,

- individuals who just don't want help,

- arrogant people who speak "rudely",

- private people who don't talk much,

- people who just want to talk about anything but their needs,

- people who just want their questions answered, not to be asked questions,

or

- people who say they just want the best advice.

However, your success requires that you get conversational, build rapport, and learn about the client's S.P.I.C.E[3] with these clients as well. You need to find ways to get past these barriers. So the important question you have to confront is, "Are you going to develop the skills that make it easier to get past any roadblocks your clients put up?"

DEALING WITH GRUFF/BELLIGERENT CLIENTS

Some clients can be gruff in their responses to you – curt, offering non-verbal signals suggesting they won't be very cooperative, maybe even making statements to you that feel like criticism. In such cases, you probably need to use the powers of perseverance and patience. Use a comeback that catches the client's attention.

CT: "Look. I'm just here because my wife said I had to come." (*said with a touch of irritation*)

CR: "Well, that's okay. We can just visit, have coffee and a snack, then spend time chatting so you can tell her you came and we talked. I'm curious – why do you think she sent you?" (*makes eye contact and smiles*)

CT: "I think she just wants me out of the house. She says since I lost my job I've been useless."

CR: "She's concerned about how you're feeling, worried you've lost your sense of purpose?"

CT: "Yeah. I don't know what to do with myself. I mope around. She gets worried."

The client tried the brush off in a gruff voice but warmed up to the eye contact, smile and the offer of an alliance to counter the pressure the client felt to be there.

The counselor did what it took to get the client talking. The counselor neither argued with the client, nor did he quit. He hung in, made a response to capture the client's attention, and began a deeper conversation.

Persevere, use patience, stay calm, have a bit of a playful smile on your face and relish the challenge. Find some way to respond to any gruff or critical comments. Find a way to get the client's attention without overtly disagreeing.

How can a counselor respond to a client who is critical about the counselor's ability to be helpful, or challenges the counselor's expertise?

CR: "Welcome to (*name of your agency, organization, or group*). My name is (*your name*). I'm glad you were able to make it to our counseling session today. How can I be of assistance?"

CT: "You probably can't. Looking at you, I'm pretty sure you've never had Crohn's disease and have no idea how debilitating that can be."

CR: "That's true, I've been fortunate with my health. I gather you've had Crohn's for a while now and you're fully experiencing chronic pain, diarrhea, and abdominal cramping?"

CT: "Yes, and the doctors have tried everything. So how are you going to be able to help me if they couldn't?"

CR: "I appreciate how frustrating and discouraging this can be, on top of the pain, anxiety and inconvenience of having to live with the disease. I can't treat you medically but I'd like to know more about what you currently do to make living with Crohn's a little more bearable?"

CT: "Well, I don't go out much and when I do, I..."

Predominantly, the counselor maintained her personal confidence, and appeared to agree with the client ("That's true."). Instead of arguing with the client, she demonstrated her own comfort with a conversation about the client's experience. By acknowledging the client's likely symptoms, the counselor earned some credibility. This is just the start of a much larger conversation about the client's S.P.I.C.E.[3].

Clients can say things that might provoke a defensive response. Remain calm and simply meet whatever response the client gives you with a persistent intention to make sure he or she gets ready for a positive change and finds the right solutions for his or her needs.

CR: "Bill, my name is (*your name*) and I'm a counselor here at (*name of your agency, organization, or group*). I'm glad you felt okay about coming to see me. How're you doing today?"

CT: "I was doing fine until I discovered they assigned a wet-behind-the-ears kid to help me deal with my issues."

CR: "Yeah... I noticed the shock on your face when Tammy first brought you to my office. I'm guessing there's thirty years of difference in our ages?"

CT: "At least. And you have no idea what it means to be in my shoes!"

CR: "You're probably right. I don't live on the street. I don't have to struggle to find a warm place to bed down at night, go without meals too damn often, or worry about my own safety. So I can't know what that feels like unless you tell me your story.

CT: "Yeah?"

CR: "Yes, I'll do my best to understand if you share what's happening out there, and I'll work with you to find ways to make it better, if you want to do that."

CT: "Well okay then. I've been moving around a lot since the city rousted us out from under the bridge. I..."

This counselor showed empathy for the client's irritation over being saddled with such a young counselor who obviously wasn't a street person. In speaking about the typical problems of the homeless and saying she didn't have those issues, she gave the client a reason to tell her about his experience. As a result, the client began to tell her how he was living. This opened up a conversation to clarify his S.P.I.C.E[3] and get the client into a state of readiness for change.

If, on first contact, a client responds with a gruff, curt or rejecting comment, hold your defensive reactions in check. Remember the client's response isn't really about you. It came from assumptions about you as a counselor, and those assumptions are incorrect if you intend to use the "GET STOKED & ACT" counseling approach. You're not going to do something to the client, which he or she would have to resist. You're going to do something with the client, supporting him or her as you engage in creative problem-solving.

Meet the client in his or her moment, paraphrase to be sure you understand what he or she is saying to you, and maintain confidence that you can be helpful. Explain your intentions. Hang in there.

DEALING WITH QUESTIONING CLIENTS

Some clients will just pepper you with questions. This might seem like a good thing in because it's an opportunity to give answers that appear to be important to the client. However, if you don't learn about the client and his or her specific S.P.I.C.E[3], you can't know if the information is truly useful to the client, or if the client is focused on the wrong issues. And when you don't get your client's S.P.I.C.E.[3], the client doesn't get ready for real change.

You would do better by turning these questions into an opportunity to engage in a conversation.

CR: "Hi there. My name is (*your name*) and I've been assigned as your counselor. What led you to want to visit with a counselor today?"

CT: "Well, actually, I just wanted to know if your agency could help me get into a methadone program?"

CR: "You're dealing with an opioid addiction, and want to get into a program to help you kick your habit?"

CT: "No. I don't think I'm addicted yet but I wanted to know what my options are. Some places offer a safe injection site. Do you guys do that here?"

CR: "Yes. However, to qualify, you have to be clearly addicted to opioids and we have to know a lot more about your needs?"

CT: "Well, I'm not there yet. How do you decide when someone has an addiction?"

CR: "Qualification for that program depends on usage, the degree of dependence, how a person is dealing with the addiction, and how a person is currently getting opioids."

CT: "That's good to know. Can a person get multiple injections every day or is it restricted to small doses in the mornings?"

CR: "Well, each person gets assigned a plan based on his or her needs. For you to be able to get into the program, we have to talk about your own situation. Please tell me about your own opioid use?"

CT: "Well, I only use it when I get ..."

The counselor answered the client's questions, but each time he followed with a question of his own, trying to get the client to talk about himself. In this step, the counselor meets the client in the client's moment by answering the questions but the counselor is also trying to lead the conversation to a discussion of the client's S.P.I.C.E[3].

Throughout this example, it's important to notice what the counselor didn't do. He never said anything critical about the client's interest in methadone or safe injection services, and never criticized the client for not answering the counselor's questions. He just demonstrated that he wanted to learn enough about the client's needs to help find the right solutions.

* * *

As you can see from the examples above, for the "GET STOKED & ACT" counseling model to work, the counselor needs to engage each client in a comfortable, open, and personal conversation. Build your skills for doing this so you're particularly able to do this with "tough" clients.

These are clients with whom almost everyone else is probably failing. These clients have developed their skills for keeping the upper hand in their interactions with counselors and other helpers. However, they are people who would likely most benefit from working with an insight-oriented counselor.

Putting the following strategies into action with "tough" clients will usually help you get past the barriers they erect and take you to a more constructive and open conversation:

- **Persist** – hang in there, don't just back off when the client tries to distance him or herself from you.

- **Align yourself with the client** – validate and identify with the client's feelings, thoughts and needs.

- **Meet the client in his or her moment** – answer any direct questions asked by the client, agree with his or her concerns, and react conversationally to anything the client says or does.

- **Show empathy** – paraphrase what the client says and reach for full understanding.

- **Use humor** – diffuse any tension between the client and yourself with eye contact, a smile, and a humorous reply.

- **Establish expertise** – humbly but confidently say things to show you know your stuff and can address the client's needs.

- **If necessary, cause some doubt** – suggest there may be more to think about than just what the client is presenting as questions or statements.

- **Explain your intentions** – indicate you would like to ask some questions, explain why, and ask permission to do so.

- **Ask S.P.I.C.E[3] questions** – ask a question to learn about the client's situation, and then ask again if the client doesn't freely volunteer information.

- **Use rapport building skills** – use specific communication skills to achieve your client's trust and willingness to talk with you.

RAPPORT-BUILDING SKILLS

Your main goal at the Engaging step is to build rapport and induce the client to enter into an open conversation with you. There are specific communication skills that do this.

INVITATIONS

An invitation is a specific request for the other person to tell you something about him or herself. Your goal is to keep the client sharing information so you learn about his or her needs. As examples of Invitations, you could say,

"Gosh that sounds interesting. Please tell me more about what it means to (*whatever experience the client might have alluded to*)?

or

"I don't know how you do what you do – can you please tell me more".

or

"Please explain what you mean when you say (*and then quote using the words the client used*).

or

"That's interesting, I sure would like to know more."

or

"Please tell me more about (_whatever you need to know about your client's situation and experience_)."

EXPLAINED INVITATIONS

Alternatively, you could use the more elaborate skill of Explained Invitations. In some cases, people might ignore your invitation if they don't understand why they should tell you more. The client might not yet appreciate your interest in helping him or her to better understand the client's full set of needs. Give the client a reason.

Explained Invitations

A statement of the importance of the information you need in order to better understand.

+

An invitation to tell you more and give you more information

First you explain why you want to know more, and then invite the other person to tell you. Be curious about his or her story and explain your curiosity. Get the client talking and telling you what he or she thinks is relevant. For example,

"That sounds important and might influence what needs to happen. Could you please tell me more about that?"

or

"It's critical I understand the real problem you're trying to solve. You've said you have a problem with (_whatever the client has suggested is a problem_). Please tell me more about how you experience this issue?"

Your explained invitation makes it easier for the client to understand your reason and to give you more information.

PARAPHRASING

Paraphrasing is the act of rephrasing what you think the other person means and then asking if you understand correctly. Give the other person a chance to correct you so he or she can expand on what is being said.

Paraphrasing

A statement that shows what you think the other person meant by what he or she said (your interpretation of the meaning of the other person's words).

+

A check-out question to determine if you have understood correctly.

Paraphrasing is a particular skill with a powerful role in the "GET STOKED & ACT" approach. Paraphrasing is an active listening skill. You don't just listen passively to the other person's words. Also, you don't just repeat back what the client said. Repeating is being like a parrot. Parroting is annoying. Think of how annoying the kids' game is when a child keeps repeating back exactly what has just been said. Instead, share your **interpretation** and ask if you have interpreted accurately.

You interpret the meaning first and then you reflect back your interpretation and ask if it's correct. For example,

"I think you're saying that....   Am I understanding you?"

or

"It seems like you mean....   Am I right?"

or

"Sounds like you want...   Is this correct?"

or

"From what you've said,
I'm guessing you mean....   Correct?"

Paraphrasing is reflecting back the full interpretation of what you get so the other person can correct you if you don't understand properly.

Typically, we interpret what a person is saying based not only on what the other person says but also on how he or she says it, what we already know about him or her, our own history, and the context in which the other person says what he or she says. In addition, we have personal filters that adjust the message as we take it in. Our values, attitudes, prior experience, perception of the situation, needs, assumptions, mood and emotions all affect our ability to understand what is being said to us. With so many influential variables, there is a good possibility that we could misinterpret.

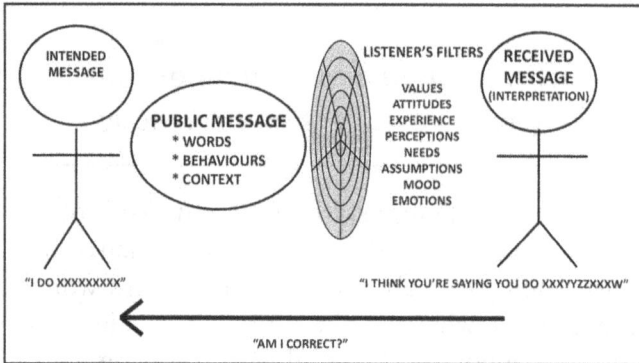

Our interpretation is usually much larger than the words the other person uses. As a result, our interpretation could match what the other person intended to convey in the way of meaning, be close but not quite what the other person meant, be completely inaccurate, or be more than the other person intended but still accurate.

There is almost always a gap between what the other person says and what we think he or she means. So we have to check to see if we have interpreted correctly. For example,

"Do you mean your loss of employment has not only been depressing for you, but also distressing for your whole family?"

60

The client can then do one of four things:

- Acknowledge the accuracy of your understanding – "Yes, that's what I mean."

- Correct the inaccuracy of your understanding – "No, what I meant is ..."

- Expand on the accuracy of your understanding – "Yes I meant that and also ..."

- Acknowledge your accuracy and expand on his or her own thinking – "Yes and that reminds me, I..."

Any of these responses lead you to full understanding because the information is clarified and expanded for both of you.

INFERENCE CHECKING

Inference checking is a skill that uses our natural tendency to form impressions about the other person. We make guesses, somewhat informed by what the other person tells us, how he or she is dressed, what the other person does, and what he or she doesn't do or say.

Normally we just act on these guesses and assumptions as if they are true. Unfortunately, we can often guess wrong about the other person and this can lead to confusion, misunderstandings, tension and even conflict.

The skill of Inference Checking allows us to find out if the guesses we make about this other person are accurate. This requires that you pay attention to the inferences and assumptions you're making about the other person.

You disclose the guesses you make in order to check if your guesses are accurate, to keep yourself on track, to learn more about the client. If you didn't check, you could be forming the wrong impressions, thereby leading you to misunderstand your client's full S.P.I.C.E^3. That misunderstanding could lead to less effective problem-solving in the following steps.

Sharing your inferences has the added benefit of allowing the client to give you more information about him or herself. The client does this as he or she either confirms the accuracy of your guess, or corrects you. In turn, if you surface something important that expands the client's understanding of his or her own S.P.I.C.E³, the client achieves greater self-understanding.

Inference Checking

> **A statement telling the other person what you infer or guess about him or her based on what you have seen or heard from the other person or have heard about him or her, or otherwise know about his or her context.**

+

> **A check-out question to determine if your inference or guess is correct.**

To check your inferences, tell the client what you infer or guess about him or her then check to determine if your inferences are correct. For example,

"I'm guessing you ....   Am I correct?"

or

"It's my inference that....   Is this right?"

or

"Perhaps you...   Correct?"

or

"I'm thinking you want...   Am I right?

Inference Checking works best when you make positive guesses about the other person, and not judgmental or critical guesses. Use your intuitive ability to form positive assumptions about your client and then check to see if your assumptions are correct. When Inference Checking with your clients, you could say something like:

"My other clients have used local shelters to get through cold nights. I'm guessing you've been doing that as well?

or

"Jill, you have five children, all under ten and you're a single mom. I'm guessing you've found ways to get the older kids to help you with the younger kids. Am I correct?"

or

"I'm assuming you're currently unemployed, have been for awhile, and you've found various ways to cope?"

or

"I'm guessing you're new to the city and don't know what community resources are available to help you deal with this. Am I correct?"

The client can make any of the same four responses as he or she would in response to a paraphrase – acknowledge you understand; correct you; acknowledge you sort of understand and then expand; or acknowledge and add any new information triggered by hearing your inference.

FEELINGS CHECKING

Feelings Checking is similar to both paraphrasing and inference checking but is focused on the client's underlying emotions. You want to focus on those underlying feelings because they're clues to your client's true motivation.

Feelings Checking is the act of showing you have empathy for the client by noticing how he or she seems to feel. You make your guess about the underlying emotions based on observations of the other person's behavior.

You naturally listen to voice tone and tempo, watch for facial, body and hand gestures, notice what is said and not said. Your mind is always trying to get a sense of how the other person is feeling based on these observations. Use that natural inclination to add to your understanding of the other person. The Feelings Checking skill is used to determine if you're reading your client's feelings accurately.

You state your guess as to how the client is feeling, and ask if you've guessed correctly. Your guess is about the other person's emotional state so your guess should be an emotion word – happy, sad, disappointed, frustrated, anxious, hurt, excited, angry, tense, stressed, eager, pleased, etc.

Feelings Checking

> **A statement telling the other person what you infer or guess about the other person's feelings based on what you have seen or heard from the other person or know about his or her situation.**

+

> **A check-out question to determine if your inference or guess about the feelings is correct.**

For example,

"I'm guessing you feel… Am I reading you correctly?"

or

"It seems like you feel… Am I right?"

or

"You're likely feeling… Is this correct?"

or

"You're feeling … about that?"
 (*clearly expressed as a question*)

When feelings checking with your clients you could say something like:

"As I listen to you, I sense a confusion about what your wife expects of you, am I right?"

or

"You seem quite frustrated by not being able to get a job that uses your skills, is this correct?"

or

"You look somewhat shocked by this calculation of your current costs. I'm guessing the size of that cost startles you?"

Once again, the client can acknowledge that you're accurately reading his or her emotions; correct you; acknowledge some understanding and expand; or acknowledge and add new information stimulated by the client's expanding awareness of his or her own feelings.

IDENTIFICATION

Identification is also an active listening skill. It's used to show the other person you understand his or her situation because you've been in a similar circumstance yourself, or you can at least imagine what it must feel like to be in the same predicament. Identification shows empathy. This will help the other person open up to you. We have greater trust in people who understand what it means to "walk a mile in our shoes".

Identification

> **Your description of your own similar experience and the feelings that you had, or your guess about how you would feel if you were in the same situation as the other person is experiencing.**

+

> **A check-out question to determine if the other person feels the same way.**

Using identification, you think of a time when you were in a similar predicament, or you imagine yourself in the other person's situation. Then check your own awareness of how you would feel. Imagine you work and live in similar circumstances, you have the same goals, you have the same problems, and you can't solve your difficulties until you get a new solution. Then ask yourself, "How would I feel if this were me?"

This is a powerful tool you would use no more than once or twice in your conversation to show empathy and caring. For example, you could say something like,

> "I remember when I finished school and wasn't able to get a job. I had to go on social assistance and lived out of a youth shelter. I felt lost and confused about my future, wondering what I could do to get back into the mainstream. I guess you feel the same way right now. Correct?"

or

> "If I imagine myself in your situation, having just been laid off at work and kicked out of the apprenticeship program, I'd feel scared about my future. Are you feeling that way?"

or

> "Janet, when I was first diagnosed with Lupus, I had no idea what that meant and felt scared because the doctor said it was very serious and hard to treat. I'm guessing you feel some of that fear right now, correct?"

or

> "Jeff, I haven't experienced what you have but when I imagine myself in your situation, I think I would feel hurt, scared, and extremely frustrated. I'm guessing you feel that way yourself. Am I correct?"

Clients will appreciate your effort to put yourself in their shoes and feel what they feel. If you guess correctly, you expand the trust and rapport within your relationship. If you guess incorrectly, the client will still appreciate your effort to understand what he or she is experiencing and will correct your misunderstanding. As the client corrects you, he or she expands his or her awareness of real feelings, and this increases your client's motivation to do something about these feelings.

EFFECTIVE QUESTIONING

Although you would primarily use the empathy skills of invitations, paraphrasing, feelings checking, inference checking, and

66

identification, there are times when you will have to ask a question to get information you need to know. Ask different types of questions. The type of question you ask has an impact on the quality of answers you get. Open questions solicit larger answers. Closed questions get single word answers.

A Closed Question such as "Do you use the services of the food bank?" will likely elicit a single word answer of "Yes" or "No". You could easily get that information and much more by asking an Open Question such as, "How do you currently feed your family?"

There's another way to classify question types – direct versus exploratory. Direct questions seek a specific piece of information. For example, if you work as a distress-line counselor, you might think to ask, "Do you have a specific intention to commit suicide right now?" This focuses the client's attention on that specific thought – a specific intention to commit suicide.

On the other hand, exploratory questions seek elaboration and an expanded story. For example, "What have you been thinking about that caused you to call the distress line this evening?" This question is more open in nature and invites a sharing of information by the client that could cover a broader range. This allows the client to take the story where he or she thinks it should go. The broad answer could include reference to a specific plan to commit suicide or not, depending on the relevance of that information to the client.

Each type of question can be useful. You just need to pay attention and learn the proper timing for when to ask the different question types. In general, you want to ask more open and exploratory questions than closed or direct questions. There are several types of exploratory questions, and as they get the client telling you more about his or her full story, learn to use these different types.

Standard Questions start with who, what, where, when, how, and why. A standard question is an open question seeking an elaborate answer. When you ask, "How do you do this now?", you're asking a standard question.

Status Quo Questions try to get an elaboration of the client's current situation. For example, you could ask, "How is your day-to-day life affected by your current (_whatever circumstance the client is_ *dealing with*)?" This is a good type of question to help you to learn more about how the client experiences his or her status quo.

"Best Of All Possible Worlds" Questions ask the client to imagine the best possibility and describe what that would look like or entail. For example, you could ask, "If I had a magic wand and could grant you what you wish for, what would that wish be?" This is a good type of question to use in order to learn about your client's expectations and excitements.

Assumptive Questions start with a positive assumption about the client then finish with a question that relates to that assumption. This works best when you assume the client has done what you think should have been done in the situation, and ask the outcome. For example, you could ask, "When you asked your partner to solve that issue, what happened?" or "When you did (*what the client could have done*), what took place?"

Multiple Choice Questions help your client to answer a question by giving several answers to choose from. Give the other person several possibilities and then ask which might apply for him or her. When people have choices, they feel more freedom to speak. As an example of a multiple-choice question, you could say,

> "I've noticed that my clients tend to deal with their homelessness in different ways. Some of them choose to use the shelters. Some of them find shelter in building doorways or in back alleys where ever they can find a shelter or box to crawl under. Some choose to live in the bush camps under the bridge, while others struggle to continuously find friends that can put them up for a night or two. What do you do?"

or

> "When looking for employment, some people use the want ads in the paper, some use private on-line employment services, some have a hangout place where people get temporary day jobs in the construction industry, and a few use the federal employment insurance office. Which works best for you?"

or

"Have you noticed if this is affecting your health, your outlook on life, your sleep patterns, your motivation to get out of bed in the morning, or your relationships with others?"

Alternatively, you could help your client to answer by asking an explained question.

Explained Questions start with a clear declaration of your reason for asking a particular question. This gives the other person a reference point to better understand the reason for giving you the information.

Explained Question

A clear statement of the full reason
that you wish to ask a question.

+

An open question to draw out all of the
other person's thoughts in response to
your need to know that information.

To use this skill effectively, you must first understand your real reason for asking a particular question. This requires an expanded awareness of your own motives and your own requirements for certain bits of information. Consequently, you should have a specific purpose behind each question you ask. It helps if you intend to learn the client's S.P.I.C.E[3] as this structure gives you the reasons to gather specific information.

As an example of an **Explained Question**, you could say,

"In order to help, I'd like to know more about any symptoms or problems you experience right now. Have you noticed any particular difficulties when you are (*doing what the other person does*) ?"

69

or

"In order to understand your goals, I need to know what you hope to gain by working on this problem. What benefits are you looking for?"

* * *

In general, ask exploratory questions at the beginning to open up the conversation. This allows your client to tell you his or her story without the distraction of your specific questions. It increases the likelihood you will learn all you need to know instead of getting focused on only part of the story.

Questions take control of the conversation and can distract the client from telling you the story in the way he or she wants to tell it. If you ask too many questions, you run the risk you will not get the whole story. You may get answers to your questions, but if you failed to ask the right question about a key aspect of the client's story, you don't achieve full understanding. Questions are necessary but you only want to ask a few.

In effective counseling, making good use of the questioning skills is an art. Know:

- when to ask a question,

- what to ask about,

- how to choose the type of question to ask in order to make answering the question easier for the client,

and

- when to use the active listening skills instead.

Experiment with different questions and different question types. Notice how your clients react. Pay attention to their non-verbal responses. Do you see your client relax as you ask the question, or get tense? Does the client move toward you ever so slightly, or move back? Does he or she show excitement about answering the question, or suspicion? If there is any hesitation, or apparent reluctance, there may be a problem with your question. Shift to using one of the other active listening skills.

MATCHING

If you really want to build rapport with another person, if you really want to show you understand, if you really want to get into the other person's shoes to achieve full understanding, then subtly and gently use the skill of matching. This is a skill best used only after you've mastered the preceding skills.

The skill can be used deliberately to achieve and deepen rapport. Rapport helps your client to feel comfortable opening up with you. Matching works when your matching behavior is below the other person's conscious awareness.

Matching involves subtly adopting some of the gestures, posture, voice tone and tempo, eye movement patterns, and words and phrases used by the other person. The key word is "subtle". You match enough but not too much.

Matching is an act of mentally becoming the other person, stepping inside his or her shoes to see and feel the world the way he or she does. When done properly and with a positive intent, matched behavior feels familiar. Familiarity leads to trust and rapport. This enhances one's feeling of safety.

Used incorrectly, the client can be put off, sensing he or she is being mimicked or even mocked. Matching isn't mimicry when done effectively, but it typically is when done poorly. If people think you're copying them, they can become suspicious. This is particularly likely if you're not genuinely trying to experience the world the way they do. Hence you want to use this skill carefully and preferably naturally. Get into a state of rapport with your client by using the active listening skills, and subtly continue the rapport building with matching behavior.

Before you actually try to use the skill, check out the validity of this skill as a natural form of human behavior. Start paying attention to conversations. Do this in informal situations where friends chat with each other or when family members engage in conversation. Watch two people who seem to be comfortably engaged in supportive conversation. First watch one person's behavior and then watch for similar behaviors as the other responds.

71

When in rapport, you will notice similar gestures, pace, voice tonality. Posture will likely be more relaxed and involve a forward lean toward each other. Conversely, when not in rapport, pace of speech might be disparate, gestures dissimilar, body posture closed and distanced from the other person. Our body language says something about how open, safe, and close we feel to the people we talk with.

Alternatively, pay attention to your own conversations with a friend. Particularly notice how the two of you look and sound when you think you experience trust and rapport with each other. If you have rapport, you will see similarities in your posture, voice tone and pace, gestures, eye movement, and word usage.

Matching must be done with a desire to empathize with, understand, and respect the other person. If your intention is to manipulate in some way, it likely won't work. Use this normal human behavior to deepen your relationships with your clients. Use matching to step into the other person's world and better understand his or her needs.

FINDING YOUR OWN WAY TO ENGAGE

You have to have your own engagement strategies. Greeting and then Engaging should only take a few moments but they are very important moments. You need to achieve engagement with each of your clients to get them talking about their needs.

It can be done. Develop your ability to react effectively to the difficulties some clients put in the way of getting into a conversation. It's up to you as the counselor to get over, around and through client roadblocks in such a way that the client ultimately wins by sharing his or her S.P.I.C.E^3 with you.

If your best efforts to get engaged in an open conversation aren't working, improve your engagement strategies and skills. Don't blame the client if you fail to do so. As I've listed above, you have some options to use when the going gets tough.

On the other hand, you're wasting time – yours and your client's – if you engage in long non-S.P.I.C.E^3 conversations. You want the conversation to be more than socializing. Make these conversations relevant counseling conversations by inducing the client to open up and tell you about his or her needs. Transition as soon as you reasonably can to learn the client's S.P.I.C.E^3.

WHEN TO MOVE TO THE NEXT STEP

You'll know it's time to move to the next step when you've completed your introductions and addressed any client concerns about your creditability or the counseling service itself; when the client appears to be somewhat comfortable with you in this counseling session; when you've achieved some degree of rapport with the client; and, when he or she is starting to share something of his or her story.

The Greeting and Engagement can take only a few minutes if the client is comfortable with both you and the idea of going through counseling; or longer if the client has strong reservations. Deal with the reservations by showing respect and empathy, by disclosing important information about yourself to help your client trust that you can be helpful, and by being more resistant about leaping into the counseling process than the client is. You can show that resistance by hesitating to move forward until the client clearly says he or she is ready.

TRANSITION TO THE NEXT STEP

Once your client is engaged in an open conversation with you, steer the conversation to a discussion of his or her S.P.I.C.E^3. To do so, ask a transition question to move the focus on to what brought the client to your agency.

"So please tell me more about what led you to contact our agency and ask to see a counselor?"

or

"I'd like to understand your situation better, particularly any concerns you might be having as you deal with (_typical problem for which your agency provides support_). Can you tell me more about your own experience with that issue?"

or

"For me to be helpful, I need to know more about what happened. Please tell me about (_how the client is currently_ *dealing with the typical problems that bring clients to your agency*)?"

or

"What problems are you having as you deal with (*whatever your typical clients have to deal with*)?"

or

"Have you been struggling with (*whatever your typical clients have to deal with*)?"

or

"I would really like to understand more about how you're coping with (*typical issues facing the client's that come to your agency*). Please tell me about your situation?"

You want your transitional question to remind the client he or she had a purpose for coming in to meet with you. The client has problems he or she is struggling to deal with. The client is both looking to counseling for help and holding a degree of resistance because change can be scary. Your shared purpose is to find the solutions your client needs in such a way that he or she welcomes that change. Your transition should lead right into that purpose.

Step Three – Take Time To Get The S.P.I.C.E³

In order to help a client get ready for real change, and to achieve a valuable definition of the client's problem(s), you both must come to know your client's S.P.I.C.E³:

- his or her situation,

- his or her problem(s),

- the implications of those problems,

- the constraints that have prevented problem-solving before now,

and

- his or her expectations and excitements about what he or she could achieve if those problems were solved effectively.

Otherwise, you could just be listening to a story of complaint or frustration that has no structure, no freeing quality, no insights, and no change value for the client.

Insight Potential When Getting The S.P.I.C.E³ – The client may be quite surprised when he or she uncovers information about the problem that had been previously ignored, denied, subconsciously repressed, or avoided because there was too much discomfort associated with that information. The client might feel a deeper sense of concern as the implications and constraints are examined. The client is likely to discover it's better to act for change now than it is to do nothing.

Steer this conversation to an exploration of the client's needs (his or her S.P.I.C.E^3). Endeavor to elevate your client's insight about what has to change. In the second step, you were building an open relationship so that in the third step, you could readily learn about your client and his or her needs. In this step, you want to shift the client to a readiness for change.

G	Greet.	Greet showing interest in the client and beginning a conversation.
E	Engage.	Engage in an opening conversation allowing trust and relationship building to occur.
T	Take Time to Get the S.P.I.C.E^3.	Initiate an open discussion of the client's needs to get his or her S.P.I.C.E^3, taking time to actively listen as the client does most of the talking while you clarify for full understanding. Reach for deeper insight.

Although Steps One and Two can happen quickly, this Step Three takes more time. Take enough time to get key information. It definitely does **not** mean you ask only one or two questions, get a few answers then launch into giving advice or telling the client how he or she can solve the problem. It also does **not** mean that you take a long time engaged in social chit-chat, just sharing stories, just visiting. This step takes enough time to fully explore the client's S.P.I.C.E^3. This is the primary step in the "GET" portion of the "GET STOKED & ACT" counseling process.

GOALS FOR – GETTING THE S.P.I.C.E^3

When discussing the client's needs, your goals are to accomplish all of the following:

- get the client to trust you,

- get the client to tell you important information, some of which he or she might not have expected to share with you, and even some of which he or she hadn't even considered as relevant to solving his or her problems,

- fully define the problem and make sure there is full clarity for what it is the client wants to solve.
  - ➢ Get a clear understanding of where the client is now and where he or she wants to be so the gap is fully understood.
  - ➢ Develop a comprehensive understanding of the S.P.I.C.E^3 in this problem situation:
    - o expand awareness of the resources residing within the client's situation, for potential use as a solution,
    - o identify and understand any symptoms and difficulties in the current situation that indicate there is a problem and clarify the cause of the problem so you're both working to solve the right issue(s),
    - o explore all of the costs (both tangible and intangible) of these symptoms and problems,
    - o clarify all of the forces, roadblocks, and constraints that keep your client where he or she is and away from where he or she wants to be,
    - o develop clarity about the minimal expectations a solution must satisfy,
    - o identify highly desirable results that create excitement in your client, and
    - o determine the deadline by which the problem must be solved.
- take your client through his or her Reality Trough, opening up the client's awareness to the emotions that reside within that trough,
- help your client to achieve new insights,
- work with your client so you both achieve full understanding of the client's needs,
- fully clarify the decision criteria your client will use to select an appropriate solution (available resources, constraints, minimal expectations, highly desired benefits, and deadline),

- build your client's eagerness to look for ways to achieve new benefits and better results than the client is currently experiencing,

plus

- establish a sense of purpose and excitement about what could be accomplished if the optimum solution can be identified.

You want to have a conversation that takes your client through the S.P.I.C.E^3 sequence to a readiness for change:

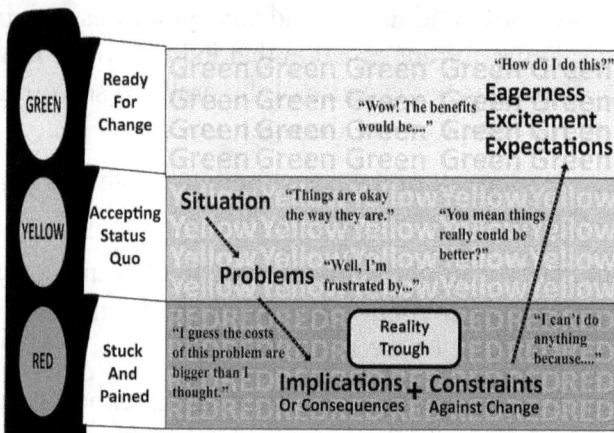

Gather information in a **conversation** as opposed to an interrogation. Your client should feel comfortable confiding to you. You want a conversational interaction where the client shares private and deeply personal information.

To clarify what I think you should be after, consider an iceberg. Only about 30% of an iceberg is visible above water while the rest is hard to discern below the water line and almost invisible. Similarly, both the client and the counselor only know a small portion of the client's S.P.I.C.E^3.

The visible information is available to the counselor by reading what might have been written down in the client's file, by looking at the client, by listening to what the client says, by noticing what the client doesn't say. The client likely knows much of that visible information, but you can't assume he or she knows all of it. The client may not be fully aware of how he or she appears to others.

As well, there is a substantial amount of information about the clients' S.P.I.C.E^3 that is likely below the client's conscious awareness, and certainly not yet known to the counselor. Some of this information has been stuffed out of conscious awareness by the process of subconscious denial. This can be either forgotten or deliberately repressed information. It's likely uncomfortable information. Step Three is all about drawing that key information out into the open, making it available to scrutiny by both of you.

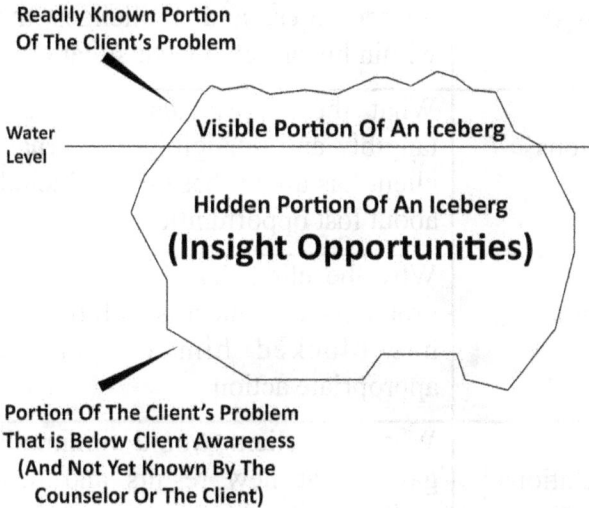

**Readily Known Portion
Of The Client's Problem**

**Water
Level** _____ **Visible Portion Of An Iceberg** _____

**Hidden Portion Of An Iceberg
(Insight Opportunities)**

**Portion Of The Client's Problem
That is Below Client Awareness
(And Not Yet Known By The
Counselor Or The Client)**

Your task in Step Three is to help your client achieve new insights about this information that is not consciously known. By doing this, you help your client clarify his or her S.P.I.C.E^3 and thereby you will both know the full extent of the problem(s) the client has to solve.

GETTING THE S.P.I.C.E^3

You need to do this in a manner that helps your client to expand his or her own understanding. You need to lead your client's awareness to the information buried in his or her unconscious mind, or otherwise ignored in the subconscious process of denial. Both of you need to learn five essential elements of the client's S.P.I.C.E^3 so the client can fully understand his or her problem(s). By exploring this information and bringing it into full awareness, you help your client to both get ready for change and to fully understand the problem(s) that need to be solved.

Situation	The client's current situation; what he or she experiences; where the client experiences what he or she has to deal with; who else might be involved; what resources the client has available to use now; how he or she copes or manages the current situation; why the client has these experiences.
Problem(s)	The symptoms, difficulties, real problems, opportunities, and challenges the client has within his or her current situation.
Implications	What these problems cost the client, both tangibly and intangibly; and what feelings the client has about these costs, including feelings about lost opportunities.
Constraints	Why the client hasn't been able to fix these problems or concerns before now; and what has blocked him or her from taking appropriate action.
E^3 xpectations, excitement, and eagerness	What the client would minimally expect to gain; what new results and benefits would really excite the client; and how eager the client is to get the problem solved (*is there a deadline?*).

Your job is to lead this exploration and draw this information out of your client. Variations of the following sample questions could be asked to uncover each of the five elements. These questions are only examples to illustrate what you want to know, because I can't write them here in a way that matches your typical client's scenario.

I would word a question differently when I'm directing it to a person struggling with an illness than I would word a question I'm directing to a person contemplating suicide, or to a parent that feels like she's lost all control over her children. You will have to use your awareness of your client scenarios to modify the wording to get at what these questions are seeking.

Learn a bunch of questions to uncover each element, but when talking with a client, only ask one, or at most two questions for each. Ask the question to direct the client's attention to the specific element, then get conversational and extend what you learn by using the active listening skills. Draw the client out so he or she volunteers more information about each element.

If you can, work through the S.P.I.C.E^3 sequence in an organized manner. Generally, you would first learn more about the client's situation, expanding on what you already know about the client from the client's file, his or her appearance, and any initial comments during engagement.

SITUATION QUESTIONS

These questions allow you to gather data and facts about the client's status quo. You need to help your client to better know his or her own situation, the people involved, and the resources within it.

- Before we talk about the problems that brought you to counseling, please tell me as much as you can about your current situation?
- I'd like to know as much as I can about you, what you like to do, where you live, friends and family, what you do well, what happened to get you to come for counseling. What can you tell me?
- What is it you experience that brought you to counseling?
- What do you think happened to bring about the difficulties that brought you to counseling?
- Please describe the context in which you experience your problem(s)?
- Where do you experience what you have to deal with?
- Who else might be involved or influenced by what you experience?
- What resources do you have available to help you now?
- How do you currently cope with or manage your current situation?

- What do you currently do to find moments of relief or respite from your struggles?
- What do you currently find helpful as you struggle to cope with your issue(s)?
- Are there any other possible resources in your current situation that you don't currently use?
- When do you experience your difficulties?

As you explore your client's situation, you will certainly learn more about your client, but the client may also have some new insights about his or her situation. The goal is to broaden the client's awareness of what brought about the current situation and how he or she is currently managing, because within the current situation, there are likely to be unused resources and key parties that will influence problem-solving success.

Situation Insight Potential - *reframing the client's perception of his or her own situation so he or she can see, hear, feel, understand the situation differently; discovering previously undervalued resources within the current situation that might be useful when a new solution is identified; clarifying further who is involved; and liberating an ability to consider new possibilities.*

Focusing on the Situation element first allows you to learn about your client's strengths and what the client is doing well. Discover how he or she is coping, what is working, and what is keeping the situation from being worse than it is. It will make it easier for your client to then consider what isn't working so well and the nature of his or her problems.

As you expand awareness of the client's current situation, the client may begin to think about the problem(s) within his or her status quo. If awareness of the problem(s) does not emerge on its own, then ask one of the problem questions to direct attention there.

PROBLEM QUESTIONS

You ask these questions to uncover the symptoms, difficulties, dissatisfactions, real problems, challenges, hopes and opportunities the client has in his or her current situation. This will likely lead your client to see and understand his or her problem(s) differently, realize problems that hadn't been recognized before, and see new opportunities not yet considered.

- What gaps are there between what you want and what you have?

- What do you wish you could achieve that you aren't achieving now?

- What about the current situation is irritating, frustrating, causing tension?

- What is the worst aspect of your current situation?

- What do you dislike the most about the way things are right now?

- What do you think are the symptoms that indicate you have a problem?

- What is the frequency of these symptoms?

- What do you think causes these symptoms or dissatisfactions?

- When did you first start to think you aren't doing as well as you would like?

- If you were to say your current way of coping could be improved, what would you improve?

Problem Insight Potential - *converting what your client previously assumed to be just normal attributes of the current situation into perceived symptoms of a problem that needs to be resolved and not just accepted; exposing the real problem when that problem has not previously been understood; discovering the underlying causes of the symptoms; determining the extent of the gap between the way things are and the way the client wants them to be; uncovering any opportunities for improvement.*

As your client discovers and clarifies problems, he or she might also get clues as to the consequences of these problems. There is significant insight potential when a client considers what the status quo truly costs. This is a critical point in your counseling process. If the client hasn't yet explored the implications, ask implication-oriented questions.

IMPLICATION QUESTIONS

These questions determine the consequences of the problems, specifically by discovering the degree of quantifiable cost, frustration, and pain the client has within his or her status quo.

- What do these difficulties and problems cost you?

- If things just continue to stay the same, what price are you paying, how much does this cost you?

- Are you encountering any particular costs because of your problems?

- As the problem(s) have continued, did the costs increase?

- If things aren't working as well as you would like, what does it cost you to stick with the status quo?

- Are there any financial or other tangible costs in continuing the way things are?

- Are there any intangible or emotional costs, such as lower morale, disappointment or frustration?

Your client needs to learn both the tangible and intangible costs of the way things are now. Ideally, he or she should know the financial implications – the real dollar costs. Quantify costs as much as possible but also notice the emotions that your client has about these costs.

By taking stock, the client will see how much not solving the problem will continue to cost. Your client's motivation to find a solution will rise if he or she concludes these costs are no longer acceptable.

Implication Insight Potential – by facing what has previously been unconsciously denied, the client will likely discover the full costs of the problem(s), suddenly realizing the consequences of not taking action are too great to live with or accept any longer.

This conversation for defining the problem(s) might now slow down because your client will likely bump up against what is stopping him or her from fixing these issues. Or your client might state something like, "But, there isn't much I can do about this." Your client now needs to focus on what prevents a solution. Get at this with a constraint-focused question.

CONSTRAINT QUESTIONS

Constraints are often the excuses the client uses to explain why he or she hasn't made a change before now. Ask questions to uncover what the client sees as roadblocks. Ask just a few of these questions to clarify what the client believes lock him or her into the troubling status quo.

- Have there been any particular reasons why you haven't made a change before now?

- Are there any roadblocks preventing you from making improvements?

- What excuses do you typically use to justify why you're in the situation you're in?

- Are there any limitations to your resources that restrict the solution(s) you could consider?

- What alternatives have already been tried or considered, and what prevented them from producing your desired outcomes?

- What roadblocks would an effective solution have to overcome?

- What resistance to change might you or others have?

There can be many different kinds of roadblocks. Constraints can be related to any of the following:

- limited finances,

- rules in place or believed to be in place that limit choices,

- reduced physical capability,

- limitations within the client's environment that restrict movement or choices,

- the client's attitudes, beliefs, and values; or the attitudes, beliefs and values of others toward the problem(s) being experienced by the client,

- a lack of skills,

- any contractual obligations,

- possible scheduling requirements,

- a low level of willingness to undergo change on the client's part, or alternatively, the client might think others are unwilling to experience change,

or

- the points of view of a significant other about what the client is allowed to do.

Part of the exploration of constraints would include a determination as to the reality of these constraints. Are they real or imagined? Ask further questions like one of the following:

- Of the roadblocks you've identified, which ones most significantly get in your way?

- Which constraint(s) do you think most get in your way?

- If you prioritize the constraints in terms of their importance, which constraints would be the most important and which constraints less limiting?

- There are times when people limit their own ability to make changes. Thinking about the constraints you've identified, are any of them just excuses and not real roadblocks?

- Does each of these constraints really exist or are any of them just reasons you think might prevent change?

Constraints Insight Potential - *identifying what is truly blocking change and what is only self imposed or imagined limitations; enabling your client to make a choice for change based on the reality of his or her situation; informing your client as to the full set of requirements the solution must satisfy.*

Once your client clearly knows what has prevented him or her from taking action before now, shift to getting the client to think about what could be possible if the constraints were removed and the problem(s) solved. Find out what he or she would really like to achieve. Discover what potential results would be exciting enough to cause your client to want to find and implement a new solution.

EXPECTATIONS/EXCITEMENT/EAGERNESS (E³) QUESTIONS

These questions are asked to learn what your client expects or hopes to achieve by solving his or her problem(s) and effectively implementing a new solution. The E^3 questions try to uncover your client's minimal expectations plus those benefits he or she really hopes to obtain. In addition, you want to discover how eager your client is to experience such benefits. The E^3 questions clarify your client's goal or goals and the deadline by which he or she wants the problem(s) solved.

- What do you minimally hope to gain with a new solution?

- What is the most important thing you want to achieve?

- If you had a magic lamp and could summon a genie to grant you three wishes, what three things would you ask for in the way of new results?

- What do you most desire or wish you could have that you don't have now?

- If we could find an ideal solution, what would you achieve that you can't achieve now?

- What do you think would be the most exciting benefit of getting a solution that would fully meet your needs?

- If it turns out that you could implement an ideal solution, what new benefits would you like to achieve?

- When do you hope to have your problem(s) solved?

- When do you need this problem to be solved?

- Is their any urgency to getting a new solution in place?

> *Expectation/Excitements/Eagerness (E³) Insight Potential* —
> *developing clarity about what the client really wants to achieve;*
> *elevating the client's expectations as to what could be achieved;*
> *bringing about a new energy and desire for better benefits; shifting*
> *motivation to an eagerness to discover how the improvement can be*
> *achieved; clarifying the deadline for when the problem must be*
> *solved; shifting from hesitation and resistance to a desire for*
> *action; and discovering new opportunities and possible results.*

The information you learn as you explore your client's S.P.I.C.E³, helps the two of you specify the criteria a solution must satisfy to be a working solution (use of available resources, constraints to overcome, deadline, and desired E^3 outcomes). This will wind up being the client's decision criteria. You do this work now so you both know what an optimum solution must be able to do. By getting this out in the open now, the client can't spring surprises on you later as an act of resistance to change by saying, "Oh that won't work because..."

QUESTIONS THEN ACTIVE LISTENING

I presented many examples of questions for each of the five S.P.I.C.E³ elements. I also emphasized the importance of only asking one or at most two questions for each element of the S.P.I.C.E³ conversation. That's because asking too many questions feels like an interrogation.

Instead, you should be primarily listening to the client as he or she shares personal information with you. Use questions like these to start the exploration of each element then use the active listening skills to draw out deeper information. Your goal is to reach for full understanding.

You achieve **full understanding** through the process of listening to the client, reflecting back what you understand from what the client has said to you, and checking to see if you have understood. You achieve full understanding when this active listening process causes the client to gain new insights about his or her problems, implications, constraints and desired achievements.

Full understanding involves three accomplishments. Your goal is to achieve all three of these important aspects of full understanding. It is not enough to achieve just one or two. Both of you must understand more deeply than before the S.P.I.C.E³ conversation and both of you must know you understand.

FULL UNDERSTANDING =

You understand the other person.

+

The other person knows you understand.

+

The other person understands him or herself more completely.

First, understand the client. Understand the deeper meaning of his or her words and behaviors. To understand all of the client's S.P.I.C.E³, encourage him or her to give you more information, and check your interpretations of that information by telling your client what those interpretations are and asking if you understand correctly.

Secondly, for full understanding to occur, it's very important the client knows you understand. Using the "GET STOKED & ACT" counseling approach, you demonstrate you understand by listening actively. You aren't just taking information in. You present back to the client what you think you're getting and check to make sure you've understood. As a result, the client knows you understand, because you actively demonstrate you do.

Lastly, to achieve full understanding, the client must increase understanding of his or her own needs. Your active listening behavior not only helps you to understand the client. It also helps the client to expand his or her own thinking and achieve a better awareness of his or her own needs. The client sees and hears him or herself more completely through what you reflect back. The client gets to re-hear him or herself through your words, form new insights and deepen his or her own self-understanding.

A key element of the "GET STOKED & ACT" counseling process is the notion that you don't move on to directing your client into problem-solving until you both fully understand your client's S.P.I.C.E^3. At least one third of the time (and more often half the time) you have available with this client should be spent on the first three steps.

Take the time to "**GET**" the information both you and your client need in order to arrive at a clear problem definition. Being any less informed before you attempt to find a solution is not an effective way to take care of your client. I propose that there is an active listening process that makes this work effectively.

Because your goal is to work through the S.P.I.C.E^3 sequence, you will likely start with a Situation Question to learn more about what your client is dealing with. Once your client has offered information, reflect back your interpretation of that information and check to see if you understand correctly.

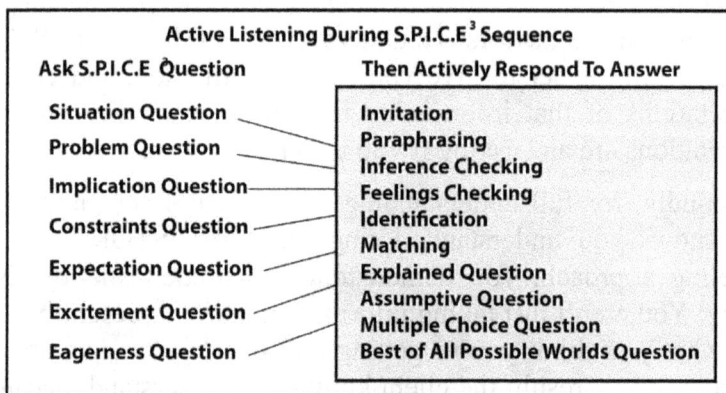

Active Listening During S.P.I.C.E^3 Sequence	
Ask S.P.I.C.E Question	**Then Actively Respond To Answer**
Situation Question	Invitation
Problem Question	Paraphrasing
Implication Question	Inference Checking
Constraints Question	Feelings Checking
Expectation Question	Identification
Excitement Question	Matching
Eagerness Question	Explained Question
	Assumptive Question
	Multiple Choice Question
	Best of All Possible Worlds Question

As the client gives information, use paraphrasing, inference checking, and summarizing to actively listen. Keep your client talking by actively following what he or she says to you. Reflect back what you receive so your client can further elaborate if you do understand or correct you if you don't.

During this process, pay attention to your client's non-verbal behavior as well as to what he or she says, because these can be important clues about the client's underlying feelings about the benefits of solving his or her problems. In turn, feelings are the windows to any subconscious and underlying expectations the client might have, even though the client may not be fully aware of all of his or her expectations.

Use the feelings checking skill to make sure you're reading the client's emotions correctly, and to show respect for those feelings. Use the skill of identification to show empathy, and to help the client feel safe in talking about him or herself.

Use Matching to enhance rapport and further put you into the client's situation. If necessary, clarify the client's thoughts about the Situation element using exploratory, explained, assumptive, and multiple-choice questions to draw out more information.

This process continues through each of the five elements of the S.P.I.C.E^3 sequence. Focus on each particular element by starting with a question appropriate to that element then clarify with the active listening skills until you know what you need to know. Then ask a question for the next element in the S.P.I.C.E^3 sequence. Get these answers in a conversation where your client does most of the talking and you listen actively.

Once your client has elaborated as much as possible in response to your use of the active listening skills, then ask a few questions to get the remaining bits of information you need. To make the questions more palatable to your client, favor the use of explained, assumptive, multiple-choice, and "best of all possible worlds" questions. Try to only ask questions to get the needed bits of information the client failed to tell you spontaneously as you actively listened.

MULTIPLE PERSON CLIENTS

In some situations, the client might be a couple or an entire family. If this is common, you will have to learn how to get all people sharing their individual perceptions of their shared S.P.I.C.E^3. The first three steps of the counseling process will be longer as you work with those involved to get all of this information out on the table.

As you move from person to person, identify the problems from each person's perspective then find out how each person experiences the implications and constraints. Learn what each person would ideally like to see as results when a new solution is applied. Help each party to achieve insights about the real problems; the true costs; the real constraints and those just imagined; plus the results and benefits that could potentially matter.

Make eye contact with each person you speak to. Use the active listening skills to check for and demonstrate understanding. It will be your responsibility to encourage all parties to listen for understanding and you will have to work harder to keep all participants moving through the exploration of their S.P.I.C.E^3 in an organized process.

Make sure each person understands you're listening to each participant so you can work together to arrive at a solution that has total support. When you think you know enough, share what you've learned about the needs of all participants. This will give you an opportunity to once more review the S.P.I.C.E^3 and make sure you have full understanding.

WHEN TO MOVE TO THE NEXT STEP

In the first portion of the counseling process, you've worked to build rapport, to earn the client's trust, and to move the client from living with his or her status quo to a readiness for change. This required your active use of the empathy skills and intensive listening. You both followed along as you listened and led the client to share his or her S.P.I.C.E^3.

You're ready to move forward when you have indications from your client you fully understand him or her, and your client has a better understanding of his or her own S.P.I.C.E^3. You're particularly ready if your client has achieved new insights.

THE TRANSITION TO THE SHIFT

Congratulate your client on developing a clear definition of his or her problem and for moving into an excitement to find a solution that results in much better outcomes.

"Bill, I'm impressed with what you've come up with – a clear understanding of what you're dealing with, the problem(s) you need to overcome, and the goals you have for what you really would like to achieve."

Then make this transition to the shift by telling your client you think you understand his or her problem(s), and it's time to get ready to do something about them. Ask for a few minutes to gather some materials together so you can prepare for the next stage.

"It's time for us to find a solution that works for you. I need time to get ready to problem-solve with you. I only need a few minutes to get my materials together."

or

"We now need to move into problem-solving to find just the right solution(s) for your needs. I think we should schedule another appointment so we have enough time to get creative and find a solution that really works. Next week at the same time okay?"

THE SHIFT

Once you've completed the first three steps, and helped your client get ready for change, you need to make a significant shift. In the first three steps, you were an active listener, drawing the client's information out into the open by reflecting back what the client offered. In these next six steps of the counseling process, you're going to take an active role in teaching the client about effective problem-solving behavior, and then moving the client through the problem-solving sequence.

Insight Potential During The Shift – If you discover the issue your client is dealing with relates to trauma or unresolved feelings from earlier in life, including but not limited to repetitive feelings of doubt, fear, anger, sadness, loneliness, obsession, stress disorder, the need to self-inflict pain, eating disorders or compulsions, and not just a clear and present practical problem, then this shift will be to use of other appropriate therapeutic methods to help your client achieve change. What follows would not be appropriate in such situations. However, knowing your client's S.P.I.C.E.[3] will help you determine which intervention is most appropriate.

The shift can happen during your counseling session or it can happen between the first counseling session(s) where you learned the client's S.P.I.C.E^3 and the next session where you will meet to engage in problem-solving. During this shift, take a few moments to review your own understanding of the client's needs, and prepare to summarize what you learned about the problem definition. Rehearse doing a S.P.I.C.E^3 summary to get ready for the next step where you will further show full understanding and explain this is the problem the two of you will solve.

G	Greet	Greet showing interest in the client and beginning a conversation.
E	Engage	Engage in conversation allowing relationship building to occur.
T	Take Time to Get The client's S.P.I.C.E^3	Get the S.P.I.C.E^3 in an open discussion of the client's needs, reaching for new insights and taking time to actively listen to the client as the client does most of the talking while you clarify for full understanding (*reach for deeper insight*).
	The Shift	*Make a mental shift from getting the client ready for change to helping the client to learn about effective problem-solving. You might also rehearse your summary of the client's S.P.I.C.E^3.*

GOALS OF THE SHIFT

You have several goals to achieve. You're going to shift your own thinking and prepare for problem-solving with your client. In the first three steps (the **GET**), you and your client focused on producing an organized understanding of the client's problem(s). Now you're going to shift to this next part of the counseling process where you will teach and help your client through a problem-solving process to arrive at a more effective solution the client will ultimately choose.

- get out any materials you will use to teach problem-solving (a note pad, flip chart, poster, pre-printed instruction sheets),

- get out any materials you will use to record your problem-solving work (notepad, flip chart sheets, pens and masking tape to post the sheets on your wall),

and

- prepare to return with an organized summary to take the client once again through his or her Reality Trough.

I've suggested you want to have materials prepared for the next steps. Your counseling environment will determine what types of materials you can use.

If you work in a large office, and have a flip chart available, and lots of wall space where you can post the flip chart paper once you have recorded key information, then use those materials. However, you may only be able to use a couple of 8.5"x11" handouts and a notepad to record information. Use whatever materials you can to make all of this information visible to your client in the subsequent steps.

THE DURATION OF THE SHIFT

The time you take will depend on how much time you have during your counseling sessions. If you have the luxury of several hours at a time with your client then it's likely you can complete the first part (the "**GET**") and engage in the remaining steps in this second part of the counseling process ("**STOKED**"), all within that session. In such a case, the shift will only be a few minutes as you gather your materials.

However, this is not likely. You might need a first session to complete the first three steps, then schedule another session to engage in shared problem-solving. In this instance, the shift might be as long as a week. Before the second session starts, and before your client arrives, get the materials ready and rehearse your summary of the client's S.P.I.C.E^3.

THE COUNSELOR DURING THE SHIFT

You have two main tasks during this shift – get your materials ready, and rehearse a summary of the S.P.I.C.E^3. It helps if you have the teaching materials prepared well in advance of all of your counseling sessions so you can use them as needed.

I recommend you always have copies of each of the following materials ready to give to your clients. Prepare these in advance then you can easily access them when you are ready to move to the next step:

- The S.P.I.C.E^3 Elements,

- The Problem-Solving Steps,

- The S.P.I.C.E^3 sheet,

- The Problem Definition,

- The rules of brainstorming,

and

- The Ideas, Elaboration and Clarification sheets.

These materials are contained within the Appendices of this book. In addition, have materials available to record the information that surfaces in each step. You want a recording media that is readily visible to both yourself and your client.

If you only have a few minutes, mentally rehearse a clear summary of the client's S.P.I.C.E^3 as you gather your materials together and set them up so the client will be able to view them. In such a situation, you'll have to multi-task as you do both – get the materials set-up and take the time to rehearse. Slow down your set-up so you can review the client's S.P.I.C.E^3 in your own mind. As well, you could possibly invite the client to go out to your office coffee machine to get a coffee or snack while you do this.

If you have more time (such as a week between appointments), I suggest that right after your first session where you learned this client's S.P.I.C.E^3, you complete a S.P.I.C.E^3 sheet (see Appendix 4). List as much detail in each section for the five elements so you have that available to you in the client's file when you prepare for the next session. Make copies of your teaching materials and put everything together with your S.P.I.C.E^3 sheet so you can easily access them at the start of your next session.

THE CLIENT DURING THE SHIFT

If the shift is just going to be a few moments long, you could direct your client to take a short break. Alternatively, you could give your client a copy of Appendix 2: The S.P.I.C.E[3] Elements, and Appendix 4: The S.P.I.C.E[3] sheet and have him or her complete the form. Have your client write out what he or she understands the problem(s) to be on a S.P.I.C.E[3] sheet.

"I'm glad we talked about your problem(s) in detail and that you feel some eagerness to find a solution. I need to get some of my materials together for the next stage, so while you wait, could you please write down what you remember about what we talked about on this S.P.I.C.E[3] sheet. This sheet (*a copy of Appendix 2*) shows you what goes where. Once you've completed it, we'll review it before we move on."

If the time frame is longer, such as a day or week, then give the client any of the following:

- instructions to reflect on what you've discussed in this last session, possibly including filling in a S.P.I.C.E[3] sheet,

- direction to notice more details that might lead to greater clarity about his or her S.P.I.C.E[3],

and

- where appropriate, some teaching material to read about effective problem-solving.

"Thank you for sharing all that information about your problem(s). It's very helpful to me, as we get ready to find the right solution for your needs. I'd like to give you a homework assignment to prepare for our next session. Please reflect on what we discussed today and write down what you remember on this S.P.I.C.E[3] sheet. This sheet (*a copy of Appendix 2*) will help you understand what goes where. I'll do the same and when we get together to find a solution, we'll start by quickly reviewing what we discussed today."

However, be prepared for a surprise when your client returns after the delay. In the first session, you worked to get the client ready for change. This can lead to change on its own as the client fully understands the status quo is not a good place to linger and change is required.

In some client situations, your client might get this new understanding and leave your counseling session determined to bring about change. Although you haven't yet worked together on what that change should or could be, the client might have formed his or her own conclusion as to what he or she wants to do.

The client might surprise you by taking some direct action to bring about change. This will lead to different results just because the client did something different. In the coming session, the client might return and tell you what he or she did and the outcomes that were achieved.

The client might be quite satisfied by that outcome. He or she might say the results are great and your client might feel there is no more need for counseling. Respect that conclusion even if you see possible problematic consequences. Let your client discover this on his or her own. The client can return to you later if he or she finds that a new problem has emerged.

On the other hand, your client might have returned to the problem situation and taken action that led to disappointment and failure. See this as your trigger to gather more information about the client's S.P.I.C.E[3] including what he or she did, what the response of others was, and what outcomes were achieved. This will likely point to more constraints and you will need to explore what they are.

If your client tried something new, congratulate your client on taking action. If your client achieved success, applaud him or her for that accomplishment. If your client experienced failure, applaud the effort and advise your client you will now work together on solving that problem with other solution possibilities.

Note: I realize what I write here presents a degree of structure you might not wish to use, or be able to follow given your own counseling situation. In many client situations you'll have to use a simpler version of this approach if you intend to do problem-solving oriented counseling. However, I've presented this structure so you can choose to use all or some of it as your situation allows.

I believe you should reach for two important outcomes – the client's problem should get solved as much as possible by the client, and the client should learn how to solve other existing or new problems on his or her own. Hence, using the materials I've proposed, you now know what you need to prepare in advance and have available to share with your clients if you want to follow this approach.

Recognizing you will have to adapt all of this to your own situation, I'll identify a simpler application of each step.

WHEN TO MOVE TO THE NEXT STEP

You're ready to move into the next part of the counseling process when you're ready with your materials and your S.P.I.C.E^3 summary. Your client is ready when he or she is anticipating what comes next.

TRANSITION TO THE SUMMARY STEP

Return to your client, ask permission to summarize what you've learned, and then in the next step, summarize what you know about the client's S.P.I.C.E^3, taking your client through his or her Reality Trough. Tell your client you want to do this to confirm understanding.

"Before we move forward to find a solution, I want to be completely sure I fully understand your problem(s). I'd like to summarize what you've told me. Is that okay? "

or

"Thank you for waiting. It's almost time to engage in shared problem-solving to find a solution you really like. Just to refresh both of our memories, we talked about... (*then move into the next step and summarize the S.P.I.C.E^3*). "

or

"Thank you for meeting with me again to engage in shared problem-solving so we can find an optimal solution that gets you the results you really want. But to make sure nothing has changed since we last spoke, I want to run through what I understand about your needs. (*then move into the next step and summarize the client's S.P.I.C.E*^{3}*).*"

Once you have the client's permission to summarize, move to the fourth step and hit the high points of his or her S.P.I.C.E^3.

Part Two – Problem-Solving To Get The Client "Stoked"

You worked on the problem definition in Part One. Now it's time to teach creative problem-solving to your client and take him or her through the process to arrive at an optimum solution or set of solutions to achieve the client's desired E^3 outcomes.

STEP FOUR – SUMMARIZE THE PROBLEM

(SUMMARIZE WHAT YOU'VE LEARNED ABOUT YOUR CLIENT'S S.P.I.C.E³)

In this step, take your client through his or her Reality Trough by summarizing what you've learned about:

- his or her situation,

- his or her problem(s),

- the implications of those problems,

- what has stopped the client from finding a solution before now,

and

- what he or she will gain by solving his or her problems.

This should highlight the client's new insights and involve a movement through the emotions of the Reality Trough arriving at excitement, anticipation, and eagerness.

Insight Potential When Summarizing *– As your client hears the summary of his or her S.P.I.C.E³, new information may emerge from his or her subconscious that expands understanding of the problem. In addition, the feelings associated with the Reality Trough will be brought to the surface again and the client might be surprised by the remaining intensity of those feelings.*

This is the first step in the problem-solving part of the counseling process. You clearly summarize the problem you discovered as you uncovered the client's S.P.I.C.E^3. The S.P.I.C.E^3 is the problem definition.

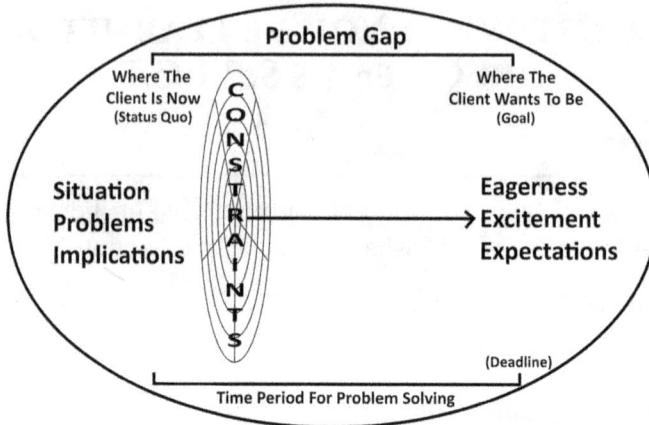

The S.P.I.C.E^3 clearly shows the gap between where the client currently is and where he or she wants to be. The S.P.I.C.E^3 shows what the current situation costs, and the constraints keeping the client from solving his or her problems. And the S.P.I.C.E^3 clearly shows the client's goals and eagerness – his or her deadline – for getting a solution implemented.

GOALS OF STEP FOUR – SUMMARIZE THE PROBLEM

At this step, you have multiple goals. You aren't yet trying to solve the problem but you're moving in that direction by making sure both of you know the client's existing needs and what an optimum solution should deliver. The goals of *Step Four – Summarize The Problem* are to:

- prove to yourself you've achieved full understanding of your client's S.P.I.C.E^3,

- prove to your client you've achieved full understanding,

- help your client realize he or she learned more about his or her needs by exploring his or her S.P.I.C.E^3 with you,

- prove to yourself your client is indeed ready for change, eagerly wanting to find a solution to his or her needs,

- teach the client about the first two steps in effective problem-solving (Feeling The Need, and Getting the S.P.I.C.E^3),

- emphasize the client's decision criteria (available resources, constraints that must be overcome, minimum expectations, desired benefits, required or desired deadline),

- create an anticipation or looking forward to the next steps in problem-solving,

and

- take your client, in an organized fashion, through the lows of his or her Reality Trough, finishing on the emotional high associated with hope and a deeper expectation he or she can gain the desired extra benefits.

Some counselors assume the client understands his or her problem(s) and jump ahead. But if the client is confused, he or she is not yet ready to look for new solutions and won't be able to make a decision for something better. If the client doesn't understand his or her own needs, there won't be motivation to change. You'll likely be wasting time – yours and the client's. It's best to do this step before moving forward in the problem-solving sequence to be sure you have a shared understanding of the problem you'll be solving.

THE PROCESS

Indicate to your client that you're now entering the problem-solving portion of your counseling process. Explain you were initially working to achieve full understanding of his or her problem(s); and you are now going to use the information you gathered to help him or her find optimum solutions that will allow your client to achieve what he or she really wants to achieve. Emphasize the importance of clarifying the problem before you try to find solutions.

Then emphasize you're going to find these solutions together. Make it clear this is a shared process. You aren't going to tell the client what he or she should do. Instead, you're going to help your client to get creative and find new solutions he or she really likes. You're going

105

to show him or her how to do creative problem-solving, and then work together through the steps to arrive at an effective solution. Declare your intention to help your client learn to do this on his or her own when future problems emerge.

Show your client a copy of the sheet with the problem-solving steps. Indicate that problem-solving began when your client felt the need to see a counselor. Feeling such a need was the first step and the client did that step on his or her own. Emphasize that the first step in effective problem-solving is to feel the need to do so. The earlier a person feels the need to solve a problem, the better. Instead of always dealing with a crisis, feeling the need earlier means less difficult problem-solving. Something led the client to come in to see you. Congratulate the client for paying attention and acting on that need.

Then explain that the second step of defining the problem was started when you worked together during your earlier discussion and you're going to continue work on that step right now. Point to the second step on the sheet that lists the steps in order. Tell your client you're both going to finish defining the problem, using the information you gathered earlier as you discussed his or her needs. You can point at the problem definition sheet (Appendix 3) and indicate that a full problem definition includes all the information about:

- the client's situation including any potential resources,
- the symptoms, difficulties, problems, opportunities that reside within that situation,
- the implications and costs of those symptoms, difficulties, problems and unrealized opportunities,
- the constraints that have prevented solving the problems or acting on the opportunities before now,
- the minimal expectations that any solution would have to satisfy,
- the exciting benefits that the client would really like to achieve if any change is made,

and

- the expected time of making the change or the deadline by which the problems must be solved.

Indicate this definition includes the client's decision criteria. The client will select a solution that uses available resources, overcomes any constraints, achieves the client's minimal expectations, also delivers highly desired benefits, and by the required or desired deadline.

If you didn't give your client a S.P.I.C.E^3 sheet to complete earlier, explain that this is called the S.P.I.C.E^3 and show your client what the S.P.I.C.E^3 elements are and what each element entails. If you didn't give out copies earlier, give the client a copy of Appendix 2.

Ask your client if he or she understands. If not, address any confusion and questions. If so, then make a shift to doing the second problem-solving step.

Note: If you had a gap of time between Step Three where you learned the client's S.P.I.C.E^3 and this session where you're going to problem-solve together, hopefully, you used that time to write out a clear summary of the five elements of that S.P.I.C.E^3, preferably on flip chart paper, and you can now post that sheet on a wall for the client to view.

Work together and summarize what you learned during your earlier conversation. Organize your summary in terms of the information that is the client's S.P.I.C.E^3 and work to surface the underlying emotions so you take him or her through the Reality Trough in the few moments of your summary. This summary should induce the range of feelings from the low point of the Reality Trough to the excitement and anticipation of his or her desired E^3 outcomes.

This summary should be brief and yet touch on the highlights of what you and your client have learned. If you took notes as you listened to your client's S.P.I.C.E^3 or if you filled out a S.P.I.C.E^3 sheet at the end of your last session, use the notes for guidance. Don't just read your notes. Quickly summarize with feeling. If learning this information took you ten minutes, give it back in crisp form within about a minute. If getting the S.P.I.C.E³ took an hour, then summarize in about five to eight minutes.

Ideally, present this in visual format. If your circumstances allow, present it on flip chart sheets you completed following your last session, or write it on flip chart sheets as you summarize. Make sure you write a brief description of each of the five elements. You could initially list what you know about each element on its own sheet, and then ask if you missed anything. This would allow the client to add anything new that comes to mind. If your situation doesn't allow for use of a flip chart, then show your client what you wrote down on your S.P.I.C.E³ sheet at the end of your last session and ask if anything needs to be added.

For best results, your summary should be brief and organized as follows:

1. Explain the S.P.I.C.E³ by showing your client the S.P.I.C.E³ elements sheet (Appendix 2) and how this information represents the problem definition (show your client the image in Appendix 3),

2. Make a brief reference to what you learned about your client's current situation. The key is to reference the highlights only, focusing on two main aspects – where in your client's situation the problems occur, and any under-utilized resources you discovered that may facilitate a solution. As the situation is well known to your client, you'll just bore him or her if you summarize too much situational information.

3. Remind your client about key symptoms, difficulties, challenges, or short comings that indicate the real problems residing within his or her current way of doing things.

4. Then summarize what those problems cost – both the tangible and intangible costs. Be really clear about each problem and the costs of that problem. Make sure to emphasize anything you uncovered that was a new insight for your client. Reducing

these costs is where the prime motivation to solve the problem resides.

5. Describe the perceived constraints that have justified not taking action before now. If you can, point out which are real constraints and which constraints appear to be imagined and not real. Say something addressing any realization that a previous concern is no longer a roadblock. Acknowledge that you both have to make sure the solution alleviates the real constraints.

6. Cover any underlying expectations your client would have about whatever he or she will change. This could include thoughts about the most important criteria the solution should satisfy, what the new solution must minimally accomplish.

7. Most critically, enthusiastically summarize the exciting benefits or results your client now expects to get. If you helped your client to achieve any new insights about what he or she would really like to achieve, stress these benefits as they are likely the most exciting to the client. Address the value of getting the problem solved now. Set up a frame of hope and excitement, where your client is eagerly waiting to find the right solution(s).

8. And lastly, ask if your client believes you've fully understood his or her needs, ask if your client thinks anything important has been missed, then ask if your client is ready to begin talking about possible solutions.

As you proceed through the summary of needs, periodically ask if you've understood everything so far. This keeps your client involved, and sets up a "yes" framework when you demonstrate you understand well. Each time he or she says, "Yes", there is a greater sense that you're working together.

Look for any clues indicating you've misunderstood or missed something. Determine if there is anything else to cover before you move on to finding solution possibilities. If so, back up to gather more information about the client's S.P.I.C.E³. Ask more questions or use active listening skills to learn what you need to know.

Let's look at an example of Step Four – Summarize.

CR: "Okay, let me summarize what I think you've told me."

CT: (*Nodding*) "Okay."

CR: "You've been living on the streets now for six months. A few times you were able to stay with a friend in his apartment where you could have a shower and wash your clothes. But this only happened when you were able to stay sober before asking your friend if you could crash for a night. A few times, he gave you some cash to get food, but pretty reluctantly. Correct."

CT: (*Head down*) "That's pretty much it. I know they have shelters available but they won't let you in if you're drunk, and even if I'm sober and get in, I'm afraid I might be assaulted by the men staying there. Plus, I need to eat."

CR: "You told me your physical health is deteriorating and you're also worried you're just slipping deeper into feelings of despair and helplessness about doing anything better for yourself. Correct?"

CT: "Yes. I'm not sleeping well. I'm getting skin rashes from being dirty all the time. I get stomach cramps from eating poorly and infrequently. I feel anxious whenever I think about approaching any agencies that might be able to help. I only came here because my friend insisted."

CR: "As well, you've been physically threatened several times and you're now worried you could die on the streets, right?"

CT: "Yes, I was cocky at first, thinking I could handle anything, but now I'm just scared. When I'm actually able to sleep, I fall asleep thinking I may not survive the night. "

CR: "You told me you don't think things can get any better because you're totally broke and can't beg or borrow money from your friend anymore. You said you can't get work because you look like such a wreck, and your drinking history meant you've lost a lot of jobs for either not showing up or showing up drunk, and don't think anyone will hire you now. You only finished grade 10 at school before you wound up on the streets and don't have any particular skills that employers want."

CT: "Right, it feels pretty hopeless most days. Especially if I can't get a drink to forget how bad things are."

CR: "You sound pretty discouraged and doubt things can get any better, but you have a bit of hope and that's what got you to come see me."

CT: "Right, I just don't want to give up."

CR: "When I asked you what you wanted to achieve, you first said you would like help finding some steady shelter – a place where you could bunk down every night and feel relatively safe. Is that still one of your goals?"

CT: "Definitely."

CR: "However, you also mentioned you would ideally like to find a room to live in where you could get cleaned up, get some decent cloths and apply for work to get a steady job. You said you'd gladly take an entry-level job if it meant you could make enough to find a small room to live in, correct?

CT: "Anything – working at McDonald's, the bottle depot, a car wash, anything."

CR: "In order to make any of these changes, you acknowledged that you need to stay sober. You'd ideally like to get into re-hab and build up your mental strength to say "no" to drinking, correct?"

CT: (*Looking at the counselor*) "Right. So what do I do?"

CR: "Helen, I appreciate that you really want change but I'm not done with this summary just yet. You don't yet think it's possible to achieve, but beyond getting sober, finding a safe place to live, and getting a job to pay for that, you'd ideally like to save a bit of money to return to school to finish your high school then go to college. When younger, you always wanted to be a nurse, and if we could wave a magic wand, that possibility is really exciting. Your dream hasn't really died, correct?"

CT: "I'd love to be able to do all that. How?"

CR: "As you think about all we've talked about, have we missed anything important in this summary of what we're trying to accomplish?"

CT: "No. Tell me what to do."

This summary takes the client through the most critical aspects of her S.P.I.C.E[3] thereby resurfacing the low feelings the client associates with the costs of being homeless and vulnerable, and then the feelings of excitement about what might be possible. The client reaches a state of eagerness, wants the counselor to tell her how to achieve this, and wants change badly. With this process, this is not a resistant client.

SIMPLIFICATION OPTION: A simpler version of this step is to just quickly review what you learned about the client's problem in the "GET" phase by saying something along the lines of:

1. "You're currently here (*describing your client's current situation and the problems within it*)."

2. "You want to be here (*describing the goal(s) your client wants to achieve*)."

3. "You need a solution by (*indicating the timeframe in which a solution is needed or desired*)."

---

4. "Correct?"

5. "Together, let's figure out how to get you what you want."

In this briefer approach, you don't have to have written summaries of the S.P.I.C.E^3 to show your client. You just summarize the S.P.I.C.E^3 verbally.

REQUISITE SKILLS

To be effective at this stage, I advise you to build the following skills:

- Hone your ability to organize the information both on paper and in your head.

- Consciously stop yourself from skipping this step until it's a habit you do every time.

- Develop your ability to summarize in S.P.I.C.E^3 chunks and ask the person if you summarized each chunk correctly.

- Get skillful at covering the highlights and the client's new insights to emphasize what really matters to the client.

- Enhance your ability to move quickly through the cycle of change as you review the S.P.I.C.E^3 so you take your client through his or her Reality Trough, first stirring up the emotions that bring about a desire for change and then placing your final emphasis on an enthusiastic summary of the benefits and gains your client hopes to achieve.

While doing this summary, you also need to use your ability to paraphrase any new information that comes up. Be patient and cover all of the important parts. Lastly, learn to recognize non-verbal cues of resistance or hesitation. If you get any, back up to Step Three in your counseling process to further discuss your client's S.P.I.C.E[3].

If you don't address any evidence of resistance at this stage, you won't be able to work with this client to find an acceptable solution. You want such issues addressed now before you make your move into the next problem-solving steps. If your client is still resisting, he or she will be an unwilling participant in all of the next steps and you will waste time – both your own and your client's.

If you detect any resistance, comment on what you see as hesitation on the part of your client, and clarify what the hesitation is about. Be persistent. There may be uncovered constraints still operating in your client's mind, or your client might not yet have any confidence the desired outcomes can be achieved. You need to uncover this information and challenge it.

If your client thinks the goals are not achievable, then work together and define goals that are. Alternatively, challenge the client's reservation and argue that you think the exciting goals are achievable, and that you will help the client work toward them, just as you will help him or her to achieve his or her minimum expectations.

Then ask if your client thinks you fully understand his or her needs. If the answer is "no", then back up and find out what you've missed. Be persistent and get that clarified. If the answer is "yes" then ask your client if he or she now better understands the need to find a solution.

Make sure the client really does acknowledge the gap between where he or she is now and where he or she wants to be. Be certain your client understands what it currently costs to stay the same. Then get your client to clearly declare that he or she wants to achieve the goals you've identified by the deadline the client indicated. In doing this, you maintain rapport and further develop the alliance with your client, as you both work to make sure you know what a complete solution must accomplish.

WHEN TO MOVE TO THE NEXT STEP

It's your responsibility to move the counseling process forward to help your client find an appropriate solution. It's not enough to just listen to your client's story, hoping this cathartic process will release pent up feelings leaving the client feeling better. Now you need to develop some creative solutions to your client's problem(s). You'll know it's the right time to move to the next step when:

- the two of you acknowledge that you have a clear problem definition (shared awareness of the client's S.P.I.C.E³),
- the client indicates you have full understanding,
- you know the client more fully understands his or her problem(s),
- the client is showing positive non-verbal clues and an eagerness to find out what he or she could do to solve the problem(s),

and

- you have a shared commitment to continue the problem-solving work.

TRANSITION TO THE NEXT STEP

This transition is simply asking your client if he or she is ready to begin the process of looking for possible solutions. For example,

"Jacob, I'm confident we can solve your problem(s), help you to achieve the goals you just set, and teach you a problem-solving process you can use in future situations. Are you ready to proceed?"

or

"Wow. This is a great opportunity – you could make a significant difference by finding the right solution(s). Shall I show you how we can do that?"

or

"Gwen, it's time for us to engage in creative thinking to identify solutions that would produce very positive results for you. This creative thinking can be fun to do. Ready for me to show you how?"

STEP FIVE: TEACH CREATIVE PROBLEM-SOLVING

The client is a survivor but probably doesn't have conscious competence using skills for creative problem-solving. As much as any other constraint he or she identified, this limitation likely holds the client back from achieving better results. It's fair to assume you have an expertise the client doesn't yet have – knowledge and skills for effective problem-solving. This is the step where you teach these skills to your client. As you teach the skills, you explain to your client what is going to happen in the next seven steps. You're going to help your client to solve his or her own problem using the skills you teach.

Insight Potential Of Teaching Creative Problem-Solving – *The client may discover there are ways to find solutions even when problems first appear impossible. The client might realize he or she has been limiting him or herself by acting contrary to the guidelines for creative thinking. The client might recognize that he or she is capable of doing what you teach. The client might come to think the "insurmountable" problem is potentially solvable.*

In this step, present the problem-solving steps to your client, then teach the skills to use at each step. Show him or her where you are in the process, and ask if he or she has any doubts about being able to do this with you.

Listen actively to any doubts. If this uncovers any perceived constraints, write them down in the constraints section of the problem definition. If this demonstrates that the client still believes the goals are not achievable, then challenge these beliefs. Answer any questions.

Your client must be both ready for change and prepared to take responsibility for finding a new solution or set of solutions. Make it clear you will help, but the client will be an active participant in the search for solutions. You will lead in guiding the problem-solving process, but the client will lead in determining what solution possibilities make the most sense for his or her needs.

GOALS OF THIS TEACHING STEP

You have several goals of your own you want to accomplish at this step in the counseling process:

- show the client the problem-solving steps, and the appropriate skills for each step,

- prepare the client for the creative thinking that will follow,

- set the stage for the brainstorming you will do in the next step,

and

- get your materials organized so you can record all ideas that emerge.

This can be a quick step in the counseling process if you prepare in advance. Have your teaching tools ready to share with your client, preferably both on flip chart paper and on 8.5"x11" sheets. Ideally, you got these materials ready during The Shift.

Be ready to post these materials on the wall or have them available on a flip chart stand so the client can see them as you review them. Similarly, have the letter size copies available to hand your client at the right time in this step.

THE PROBLEM-SOLVING MODEL

You're going to share a complete problem-solving model with your client and teach him or her what you're going to do together to find just the right solution(s). Hand your client a copy of this model as shown in Appendix 05.

This means you'll need to learn this model in advance and get used to using it to solve your own problems. In order to have problem-solving expertise to share, you need to make sure you're able to work through these steps to arrive at your own optimum solutions for your own problems.

THE MODEL YOU WILL TEACH

This model has nine steps. The client has completed the first two already – the first by getting him or herself to come to see you for counseling, and the second as you worked together to clarify his or her S.P.I.C.E.[3]. You want to emphasize this and congratulate the client for having done so.

Present the steps. Give your client a one-page sheet with the following model on it, and using your flip chart version, walk the client through the steps explaining the task at each step. Emphasize once again you have already completed steps one and two. You can start by saying something like:

> "We're going to work through the following steps to arrive at a solution just right for you. We will do this together so I'll help you to come up with ideas and find an optimum solution. However, I also want to show you how you can do this on your own for future problems. The first two steps have been completed already – the first by you when you decided to come for counseling, and the second when we met last time and sorted out what you're dealing with. The first step involves feeling the need to solve a problem." (*and continue through the steps*)

Step	Task
Feel The Need	Recognize at some level, possibly even just subconsciously, that you feel a gap between where you are and where you want to be
Define The Problem (S.P.I.C.E^3)	Sort through your own S.P.I.C.E^3. Uncover the problem, the costs of the problem, any constraints that limit your progress, expectations you have for what you would need to achieve, any desirable results you would really like to achieve, and your eagerness to get this ideal outcome. Specify the criteria a solution must satisfy to be a workable solution (available resources, constraints to overcome, deadline and E^3 outcomes).
Generate Solution Possibilities	Suspend all critical and evaluative thinking to engage in uncensored creative thinking and generate as many solutions ideas as you can in a defined time period.
Elaborate and Clarify	Look for the best attributes of each idea. Expand on ideas. Merge ideas together to make them even better. Clarify the full meaning of the expanded ideas.
Evaluate	Evaluate each idea and determine whether or not the idea meets your decision criteria.
Decide	Decide which solution or set of solutions will give you the best possible results.
Action Plan	Determine when you will do what, where, how, with what resources, and why.
Implement	Act on your decision by implementing your solution according to your plan.
Assess	Determine if the solution produced your desired results and review how well you followed the problem-solving model.

There are effective skills that can be used at each of these steps to arrive at optimum solutions. You want to talk in general terms about these skills with your client at this step, and then apply them later in the following steps in your counseling process.

THE SKILLS

Hand your client the sheet below that shows the skills to be used at each step and explain that these skills work well to achieve optimum solutions. You can start to do this by saying something like:

> "(*Name of your client*), these are the skills we will use at each step of our problem-solving work. I want to just point them out to you now and then, as we reach each step, I'll explain the skill once again and guide us through it. For the first step, you can be more effective by noticing any feelings you have that things could be better than they are. For the second step, defining the problem, you can write out your own S.P.I.C.E^3 like we did in our last session. You can use a S.P.I.C.E^3 sheet like this one (*handing a copy of Appendix 04*)."

Step	Skills
Feel The Need	Notice Your Feelings That Something Could Be Better Than It Is
Define The Problem (S.P.I.C.E^3)	Write Out Your S.P.I.C.E^3 • Situation • Problems (Symptoms, Frustrations, Difficulties, Opportunities) • Implications or Costs Of The problems • Constraints and Roadblocks • Minimal Expectations, Highly Desired Results, Deadlines

As you explain the step for writing out the S.P.I.C.E^3, you can show your client the S.P.I.C.E^3 elements sheet, and explain that these are the questions you explored in your last session.

"When we met last time, we addressed these questions to arrive at your own problem definition. We reviewed that a few minutes ago and it's posted on these flip chart pages (*pointing at the charts*)."

Then continue to explain each of the skills for the steps you will do shortly.

"Our next step would be to engage in creative thinking to generate a list of many solution possibilities. You might not be used to thinking like this but it can be done and it is usually fun to do. We will brainstorm ideas."(*and continue through the steps*)

Generate Solution Possibilities	Brainstorm Many Solution Possibilities • Set A Definite Time Period • Think Of And Say Out Loud As Many Ideas As You Can • Think Of Unusual, Far-Out, Imaginative, Even Absurd Ideas • No Evaluation • Record All Ideas • Cheer Yourself On For Coming Up With Many Ideas
Elaborate and Clarify	Complete An Idea/Elaboration/Clarification Sheet For All Ideas • Make Ideas Bigger • Merge Ideas • Guess At All Possible Meanings

Evaluate	Look At Positive Attributes Of Each Idea First Then Assess Weaknesses
	• Do Pro/Con or Advantage/Disadvantage Lists
	• Measure Each Idea Against Your Decision Criteria
Decide	Pick A Set of Solutions That Could Work Together To Produce The Best Results
Action Plan	Specify when you will do what, where, how, with what resources, and why. Record The Plan
Implement	Act on your decision by implementing your solution according to your plan.
Assess	Determine How Well You Did
	• Measure results
	• Review Your Problem-solving Behavior Looking For Strengths and Weaknesses.

Ideally, you will review this material with your client in less than 15 minutes. Your goal is not to do these steps during this teaching step but to share what you intend to do with the client in the following steps. It is like showing a map of where you're going to travel before you drive the planned route.

You can probably do this more quickly if you previously gave these materials to the client to read between your counseling sessions. However, that won't be an option available to you if your client has difficulty reading.

SIMPLIFICATION OPTION 1: A simpler version of this step would involve saying something like the following:

"Because I want you to take an active role in finding a solution to your problem, and because I want to help you to learn some important steps in effective and creative problem-solving, we're going to work through the following steps. We're going to brainstorm a whole bunch of possible solutions without evaluating any of our ideas. Then we'll expand each of our ideas making each idea a better solution before we try to determine which solution is the best. So initially, I'm going to interrupt any attempt by you to criticize ideas so that our creative juices can work. You've got a challenging problem so we need to get creative. After we've done that, we'll evaluate each idea. We'll determine if each idea overcomes your constraints or not, meets your minimal expectations, yields the highly desired benefits you want, and solves your problem by the time you need or want a solution. You okay working on that basis?"

SIMPLIFICATION OPTION 2: You could postpone the teaching and explain what you're going to do at the beginning of each of the problem-solving steps, then when you've finished all the steps, review the whole sequence.

WHEN TO MOVE TO THE NEXT STEP

Once you've shared your map of the journey the two of you will take, move to the next Step. You'll know you're ready when your client indicates he or she understands where you're going (toward his or her desired outcomes) and how you'll get there.

TRANSITION TO THE NEXT STEP

Indicate you're ready to begin the next step and ask if your client similarly feels ready to do so.

"Sam, I think we're ready to begin solving this problem. Do you share that thought?"

or

"I'm excited about working with you to find the best possible solution. Do you share that excitement? Should we proceed?"

or

"Do you have any questions about how we're going to find you an optimum solution for your problem(s)? If not, I'm ready to proceed to the next step. Are you?"

or

"Remember, I'm going to guide us through these steps and explain the skills each step of the way. I'm ready to begin. Do you feel ready to give this a try?"

or

"Okay, we've got a definition of your problem. Now we're going to find some possible solutions. I'll guide you through the steps we're going to follow and explain the skills each step of the way. I'm ready to begin. Do you feel ready to give this a try?"

Step Six:
Option Search
(Generate Solutions)

The client will be richer when there's more than one alternative to consider. In fact, the chance of finding an optimum solution rises extensively with the consideration of many possibilities. This process of generating more than one useful alternative can be fun and creative. Done right, this step will yield a surplus of ideas.

Insight Potential When "Searching For Options" – *When this step is done right, the client is more likely to discover a solution that is both innovative and superior to other ideas. When done effectively, the client moves beyond consideration of run-of-the-mill possibilities to creative thinking where the unexpected has a chance to emerge. Your client has an opportunity to achieve a real breakthrough, to find a solution that hadn't been considered before by anyone else but is obviously the best solution once it has been discovered. The client has an opportunity to invent a new way of doing what he or she does.*

You're now in the step in the "GET STOKED & ACT" model where you will help your client to search for many options (*the "O" step*). In this step, you'll show your client how to generate many solution possibilities and help him or her to do so.

Up until now, you and your client have predominantly used conscious thinking to sort out the problem. In this mindset, you sorted through facts looking for new insights about your client's S.P.I.C.E[3].

Now it's time to stimulate creative juices as you both consider a very broad range of possibilities. Suspend the focus on facts, put to sleep any critical thinking, and open up your client's mind. It's time for creative thinking, which draws on the power of the subconscious mind to open the client's awareness to many possible solutions.

The thinking of our conscious mind generally revolves around normal everyday thoughts. These thoughts are targeted at sustaining the status quo and not imagining a new and better world. The conscious mind tends to come up with typical ideas, and immediately judges them as either appropriate or not. The goal of the conscious mind is to find an acceptable solution and move on. If an idea isn't immediately judged to be a good one, the idea is discarded.

One fallacy too many people hold to be true is that they just need to identify one adequate solution and the problem is solved. It's self-defeating to come up with only one 'somewhat-acceptable' alternative in order to have the illusion that the problem has been dealt with.

The subconscious mind however, can entertain the impossible, the fantastical, and the unusual. Our subconscious is the dwelling of fantasy, dreams, imagination. We want to tap into that type of thinking. We want to open the pathway to our subconscious mind and bring into conscious awareness those creative and innovative ideas that can truly be game changers. If we expand the boundaries to include more ideas, we have a greater probability that the best solution(s) will emerge.

Solution generation is a distinct step in the problem-solving process and no other activities should be allowed to encroach on the process of just generating new ideas. During this step, you are no longer questioning whether or not a problem exists, defining the problem, or wondering what it is that your client is trying to achieve.

Similarly, you and your client are not determining which is the best idea, making a decision, or prepping to implement any one idea. In this step, the two of you are just generating a list of possible (and even impossible) solution ideas.

For effective problem-solving to occur, critical thinking must be temporarily suspended to free up our imagination and open the door for creative ideas to emerge in the same way we normally produce fantasies and dreams. By setting aside a requirement that ideas must be logical or must immediately meet a standard of good quality, the mind is allowed to form creative associations. These associations might actually be weak solution ideas on their own, but when liberated, act as a bridge to ideas that might turn out to be the most effective resolutions to the problem.

By setting aside logic and our normal critical thinking processes, we're better able to realize insight and arrive at a solution that would not normally have been considered, one that turns out to obviously be the best solution once identified. Such 'ah ha' ideas come from a different order of thinking compared to what has kept the client mired in the problem up to this point.

In this step you and your client will now think about as many solution possibilities as you can, particularly including those solutions that might appear to border on the impossible. By setting aside the need for an idea to be a good idea, your client's mind opens up and many more ideas can emerge. More ideas means more latitude to generate a solution that is very different from anything considered before.

Acey Rowe, on her CBC Radio program on December 5, 2017 shared the story of Robert L'Hirondelle. At the age of 20, he was living on the streets, down and out with health issues, harboring a drinking problem, and spinning out of control, when he got the idea to climb out of his life into a new one. He got inspiration from listening to Michael Jackson singing, "Take a look at yourself and make a change."

This led to a deep moment of self reflection in front of a mirror during which he made a commitment to change. He clarified his goals to quit drinking and end his living on the streets. He got himself to

Hope Mission and involved in counseling with an outreach worker. In this work, he found an unexpected way to turn his life around.

First he started recreational dancing, and then he entered a talent show as a Michael Jackson impersonator where he moonwalked to his own success. He quit drinking and became Edmonton's only Metis Michael Jackson tribute artist, performing for his living. Who knew when he was in the deepest portion of his reality trough that becoming Michael Jackson would be his solution?

We can't know in advance what a client's best solution is going to be. We have to work with our clients to find what works best for them, and it can be something totally unanticipated.

GOALS FOR THE OPTION SEARCH STEP

This step involves only one activity – generating many options that could be possible solutions to the problem. The goals at this step in the problem-solving process are to:

- produce a list of as many options as possible, where at least 30% of those ideas, at first glance, are very unusual, weird, imaginative, possibly impossible, maybe not even clearly related to the defined problem,

- have fun getting creative,

and

- generate options that ultimately arrive at no fewer than three optimum solution possibilities.

At this step, we aren't looking for just one solution but several of high quality, each capable of achieving the desired E^3 outcomes. To do this, we try to uncover many ideas without worrying at this stage if they're any good. We don't limit ourselves by only pursuing one solution – expand your client's opportunities by reaching for several.

BRAINSTORMING

In order to achieve the best possible solution, one that achieves the full E^3 outcomes, many novel and creative options (ideas) must be generated. The principle process for this creative thinking is called brainstorming. Brainstorming is a term initially popularized by Alex F.

Osborn in the book *Applied Imagination,* based on his work with groups working on advertising campaigns. This is now the most commonly used technique for creative solution generation. Over time, specific rules of conduct have emerged:

1. Set a definite time period for solution generation and generate ideas throughout (*Stick to that time limit*).

2. Use a time period for solution generation that parallels the significance and difficulty of the problem.

3. Think of and say out loud as many ideas as you can in the time allowed.

4. Think of unusual, far out, imaginative, even absurd ideas.

5. Suspend all censorship – there should be no evaluation or criticism of any idea during this period.

6. Record all options as they are said out loud, without censorship or modification in the act of recording each idea.

7. Record even those options the recorder might think have been expressed already.

and

8. Cheer yourself on and make encouraging comments about the growing number of options – not the quality of the ideas themselves.

Each of these rules has a very deliberate purpose. The objective is to free up your client's creative thinking, thereby increasing his or her potential to arrive at an optimum solution. Encourage your client to quickly generate thoughts and help him or her to do so. Give both yourself and your client permission to say out loud whatever comes to mind, trusting your subconscious minds to make associations your conscious minds would never consider.

Initially, there can be a delay in the flow of ideas until the client can shift mental gears. It can be challenging for some people to adopt the rule of just thinking of ideas without evaluation. Too often, people think they have to come up with a good idea. Then, they spin their mental wheels trying to think what that could be. The imposition of the critical thinking process to decide if a thought is a good idea or not, stops the flow of ideas. However, once a person can loosen up and just say out loud what comes to mind, then ideas will flow.

Encourage your client to think of unusual associations to the problem. Urge creative thinking by asking for unusual, far-out, weird, fantastical, even impossible ideas. Urge your client to think of things that have nothing to do with the problem and just say them out loud. The association with the problem may not be obvious or even exist at this time but if each of you states out loud what has come to mind, this causes other associations to form. Such associations lead to new thoughts and ideas that must also be stated out loud. Such unusual ideas liberate other thoughts and a new creative thrust takes place.

For this to work, both you and your client must suspend all evaluation. Criticism kills ideas. If an idea is immediately put to the test, of rightness then the process bogs down. This key rule of "NO EVALUATION" forces us into different thinking. Instead of critical analysis as each idea surfaces, we simply allow each idea to trigger new ideas.

Brainstorming Rules

Set A Time Limit, Stick To It
As Many Ideas As Possible
Weird and Far-out Ideas
No Evaluation
Record All Ideas
Encourage Quantity

Record all ideas exactly as they are expressed, then move on to the next idea. By recording each idea, the client doesn't have to worry about remembering the idea, doesn't have to think about its value, and doesn't have to stop generating new ideas because that idea can be reviewed once the solution generation step is completed.

In some cases, an idea might emerge which seems to just be a duplicate of something previously recorded. Record it anyway and in the exact words in which it is expressed. Excluding this idea is a form of censorship killing further idea generation.

Encourage quantity, not quality. By praising the flow of ideas, your client feels rewarded for creative and lateral thinking, and hears permission to come up with more of what the critical mind might consider to be weird, too far-out, and even absurd or impossible ideas. Cheer yourselves on to more ideas. Demand 5 more, 10 more and so on. Continuously stress the need for more ideas while there is still time to generate them.

Ideally, try to achieve an appropriate number of ideas for each problem type. You need fewer ideas to solve less important problems. You need more when the problem is seen as very difficult. For solving very costly problems where great benefits could be realized if an optimal solution is discovered, the objective should be higher. Where the problem is very important, or perceived as impossible to solve, generate as many ideas as you can, with a third of the ideas being unusual, weird, far-out, fantastical, maybe even impossible ideas.

Problem Type	Minimum Number of Ideas
Minor Problem that is not important and also seen as easy to solve	8 or more
Minor Problem that is not important but seen as very tough	15 or more
Major Problem that is very important but believed by your client to be solvable	25 or more
Major Problem that is very important but also believed to be almost impossible to solve	35 or more

To introduce brainstorming, you can say something like the following to your client:

"(*Name Of Your Client*), it's now time to generate as many solution possibilities as we can. To do this, we're going to work with some very specific rules:

131

- Set a time period and stick to that time limit. I recommend we do this for 10 minutes.

- Think of as many options as we can. I suggest we try to find at least 20 ideas.

- Think of unusual, far out, imaginative, crazy, even absurd ideas. No idea is a bad one.

- No evaluation or criticism of any idea. All ideas are good ones.

- Record all ideas – I will do that for us on this (_notepad, flip chart or computer_).

This might seem strange to you at first but it can be fun. I'll make sure we follow these rules. If you start to criticize any idea or say it won't work, I'll stop you. If I do any criticizing of an idea, you stop me. If you seem to run out of ideas, I'll stimulate your thinking by saying weird thoughts, shout out unusual words, or point at things in this office and say things like "what does that suggest we could do about this problem?" Our job is to allow ideas to come into our brains and just say them out loud. Are you ready?"

STIMULUS TRICKS

There are things you can do to shake up your client's thinking when it seems like he or she isn't contributing. Free associate. Use anything inside or outside the room as a stimulus. Look at the stimulus item and just say what ever comes to mind. Try to introduce humor – it will loosen up your client's thinking and turn this into a form of play. Get your client to do the same. By turning to such stimulants, you interrupt the stagnant thought processes that stop your client's creativity. Use these subject-changing tricks to force a new direction of thinking.

Alternatively, if you're inside, go out. If in one room, move to another. If you're working in the morning, stop and continue later in the day, perhaps at a place to eat or play.

If you notice that many solution ideas appear to be heading in one direction, then look for ideas that go in a different direction. For example, when working with a troubled parent about how he or she could bring more order into the household, and the client's ideas are focussed mostly on how to discipline the children, it might be time to throw out quite opposite ideas like:

- Let the children run the household.

- Encourage the children to bring their friends to the house for a party.

- Hold a discipline court session in which the children are the judges and the parents are to be disciplined.

- Talk about the importance of being creative, spontaneous and uncontrolled in the house so each person can find his or her true self.

- Throw out all existing rules, operate without rules until one of the children complains about the need for re-instigation of one of the rules, then have a family debate about the need for the rule.

- Have a binge session watching Speechless, a TV show about a family that prides itself on being disorganized, apathetic, and below average in everything.

- Ask your children to survey their friends to find out what rules exist in their homes and which ones the friends think are pretty important to household order.

- Ask the children to fantasize about how they would like things to operate in the house and what rules the parents have to follow.

- Spend less time in the house and do things together as a family that the children choose.

- Throw-out most of the household furniture, toys, electronics, excess clothing, and develop a minimalist lifestyle where each of you has little responsibility for possessions.

- And so on.

The objective isn't to criticize the previous ideas but to change the focus, to bring about a new stream of creativity.

You need to build your own skills and comfort with coming up with fantastical ideas. You'll play the role of stimulator rather than be the one that comes up with pragmatic, everyday solutions. So get used to thinking of weird and fantastical ideas to cause your clients to do their own creative thinking.

You want to help your client to find his or her own creative ideas. You do not want to be the only person generating possibilities. If your client is frozen, then talk about that with your client.

CR: "Bill, I notice you haven't offered any new ideas for the past few moments. What's happening?

CT: "I just can't think of any good ideas to say."

CR: "Sounds like your inner critic is interfering, that you're evaluating each thought before just saying it. What thoughts did come to mind?"

CT: "Well, I thought I could steal a car and drive to a warmer place, but I can't do that."

CR: "Doesn't matter right now if you can do an idea or not. What matters is just saying the idea and writing it down. I'm putting that one on our list. I'm glad you came up with it. Any other thoughts?"

CT: "I thought about making a sign asking for money and standing on the street. I've seen guys do that."

CR: "Good, That's now on the list. I have another idea. How about painting fences."

The goal right now is to draw ideas from your client and to lead him or her toward creative thinking. This will be a challenge, but don't assume your client can't do this. Show your own creative thinking, and then invite your client to join in the silliness of thinking of unusual, fantastical ideas. Get playful. Find your client's inner child and stimulate the unfettered thinking that children do so well.

"What do you think you might have done about this as a kid?"

or

"If you were only 7 years old, what might you do?"

Do whatever it takes to cause your client to suspend his or her critic to get playful. Stimulate your client's creative thinking by exercising your own.

SIMPLIFICATION OPTION: Instead of explaining the rules of brainstorming or talking about creative thinking, you could induce this process by saying something like:

> "Okay, we know what you want to achieve. Now we need to think about what to do to accomplish this. Right now, I just want you to think about as many options as possible and they don't have to be good ones. I just want to make a list of possibilities. Have you given any thought to what you could do?"

Then as your client offers any thought, write the idea down and say something like:

> "Great, we have one option so far. Can you think of anything else?"

Continue this process of drawing out your client's ideas. Intermittently, offer your own, being as creative as you can be. If your client criticizes any idea, then say something like:

> "You're probably correct but right now, I just want to build a list of possibilities until we find something that might really work. Instead of criticizing ideas, let's just make a long list of possibilities. Can you think of anything else?

If your client doesn't offer up an idea, then offer your own outlandish alternative. Then write it down and say something like:

> Wow, now we have a couple of options. Any other possibilities come to mind for you, even silly ones?"

Continue this until you think you have a list of possibilities, including items that seem quite absurd.

WHEN TO MOVE TO THE NEXT STEP

You'll know it's time to move on when the specified period of time for brainstorming has elapsed, or when the idea flow has stopped, which ever is <u>later</u>. Do not move on before time has expired and do not move on if ideas are still coming at a satisfying pace. More ideas help, not hurt. In fact, even if you move on and the client subsequently has a new idea, add it to the list.

If you haven't achieved the suggested number of ideas for the nature of the problem the client is trying to solve, then add more time for brainstorming and encourage more creative thinking. You shouldn't move on to the next step if you don't have enough ideas. You can move on when you have at least the suggested minimum number of ideas given the difficulty of the problem, with 30% of those ideas being weird, far-out, fantastical ideas.

TRANSITION TO THE NEXT STEP

You have a list of ideas but you don't yet have full understanding of the ideas, and the ideas are not as fleshed out as they need to be. In the next step, you and your client will work on each idea to make sure the idea is clear and the idea has been expanded to what it could fully entail.

Indicate that it's time to shift focus to clarify and elaborate each of the ideas. Do this by saying something like:

> "We've got a lot of possibilities written down but they're just idea kernels right now. We need to look at each one, clarify it, elaborate on it, expand each idea into a workable solution."

or

> "Okay, we have a bunch of idea fragments and we need to expand them, clarify them, bring ideas together to make a whole idea. We need to still think creatively as we turn each of these fragments into a workable solution."

STEP SEVEN:
KNOW EACH IDEA
(ELABORATE AND CLARIFY)

There is a normal tendency to immediately criticize and evaluate ideas, putting them up against measuring sticks such as "Is it logical?, "Is it too expensive?", "Will it work?", "Will others accept it?", or even "Do I like it?" These are important considerations a solution must satisfy before being selected as the solution, but when these questions are asked too soon, and when ideas are still immature and not fully formed, too many ideas get rejected too soon. Before rejecting ideas, you want each of you to fully know each idea – what it means, entails, could accomplish, how it could be merged with other ideas. Problem-solving is enhanced when kernels of ideas are clarified, expanded, elaborated, even added to other ideas so they're given fair consideration before being critically evaluated. Know the depths of each idea.

Insight Potential When "Knowing Each Idea" – *The strengths of initially weak ideas may emerge when clarified, expanded upon, elaborated, or added to other ideas to make a better whole, and such ideas may become an optimal solution. An idea that at first glance might be rejected has the opportunity upon deeper consideration to become the innovative solution that yields exceptional results. Expanding ideas, fleshing them out, and pulling ideas together increases the chances of discovering optimum solutions.*

By now, you and your client should have a large list of ideas – more if the problem is perceived as difficult. Most of these ideas emerged as brief thoughts and were written down as such. The full scope of each idea is not yet known. Many of your ideas may not be all that clear so it's important to get clarity before evaluating the idea in a later step. In the problem-solving steps, this is the Elaboration and Clarification step.

This is the step where you work with your client to achieve shared understanding of what the idea means, what it entails, how it would work, what it could potentially do, how separate ideas can be merged together to create another promising possibility. Once the idea has been clarified, expanded, and fully understood by you and your client, then and only then, can it be critiqued. That critique will happen in the step after this one.

Once again, delay all criticism and any attempts to select the final solution. You want the optimum solution, and at this point you only have a list of possibilities – many of which are not yet completely understood and many of which are not fully expanded ideas. Premature evaluation would kill most of them.

GOALS OF KNOWING EACH IDEA

As a counselor who wants to maximize the likelihood your client finds and implements an optimum solution, you have several goals at this step:

- Elaborate and expand on all ideas so they are seen in their best light and all potential elements of the idea are brought into awareness.

- Clarify all ideas as if they all have tremendous implications for the optimum solution of your client's problem.

- Prevent any premature evaluation of ideas that fall into the category of appearing to be too far-out, impossible, or weird.

- Inhibit rejection of ideas as unworkable before they are fully known, understood and expanded.

- Flesh out creative ideas to the degree they become optimum solution possibilities.

And whenever your client thinks the list includes too many ideas,

- Arrive at a short list of enough fleshed out ideas with seventy percent (70%) comprised of those seen as potentially workable solutions, and about thirty percent (30%) of ideas that at first appear to be too far-out or fantastical.

You're still looking for creative thinking at this step. The brainstorming mentality should continue as the ideas are clarified, expanded, elaborated and merged to make viable solutions.

Make sure your client understands and accepts this notion. He or she is likely going to feel some impatience to find something that works and you need to slow that impetus down. You may have to be the champion supporting the silly, apparently inadequate, possibly impossible ideas to make sure they receive enough attention to become real possibilities.

The primary objective is to retain and flesh out as many of the ideas generated in the Options Search step as possible so chances of finding optimum solution opportunities are as high as possible. Rejection of ideas before they're fully understood and expanded leads to loss of useful information.

STRATEGIES FOR REDUCING THE NUMBER OF IDEAS

If you were successful in the previous step and generated a large number of ideas, your client might feel overwhelmed with the number of options to consider. The ideal process would be to clarify and expand every idea. However, if your client thinks there are too many ideas and this step would take too long, then there are various strategies you can use to reduce the list to a manageable number, while saving the most creative ideas for consideration.

- Look for and cross off the ideas that were just stated to stimulate creative thinking of other ideas.

- Group together any ideas that have similar elements – work down to groups of similar ideas.

- Group together ideas that could work together to make a bigger idea.

- Cross off those ideas that have been tried before.

- Allow your client to chose at least five ideas he or she would want considered further. You do the same but pick a different five.

or

- Together, pick seven ideas that you both think could be possible solution ideas and then together pick three fantastical ideas.

Now take your shortened list of ideas and really get to know, elaborate and clarify them.

Be aware though that your client runs the risk of throwing out optimum solutions because of a premature censorship. Instead, if possible, work forward with as many ideas as you both can manage.

NOW GET TO KNOW YOUR IDEAS

At this point, you have a list of ideas to be considered further. You and your client do not have a list of solutions yet. Ideally, your client now has both creative and practical ideas to expand and clarify with no allegiances to any particular idea or ideas. You want your client to proceed with an open mind. Set out in this stage to work with your client to elaborate and expand ideas so the optimum solution(s) can emerge.

Suspend censorship, criticism, and selection until all ideas have seen enough of the light of day to be given a fair evaluation. The ideas aren't yet clear. They are just thought kernels and need more elaboration.

The guidelines for this stage are:

1. Make no selection of a solution at this time.

2. Elaborate and expand on all ideas – do not cut the process short.

3. Merge ideas that are complimentary to each other.

4. Clarify all ideas, allowing all thoughts about what the idea means to surface.

5. No evaluation, censorship, or criticism of any idea.

Presumably, you've your recorded list of ideas. It's now time to create a new recording sheet, an Elaboration and Clarification chart, which looks like the following:

IDEA	ELABORATION *(Expand Each Idea. Flesh It Out)*	CLARIFICATION *(Understand The Full Idea)*

Take the list of ideas you're going to work with and write each idea in a section of the IDEA column. Write each idea as it was expressed, taking the ideas in order from the original list of all ideas. List them all, or if you have used one of the preliminary weeding out strategies, take the remaining ideas and list them all.

Then focus your joint attention on the first idea and get the client to clarify what the idea means to him or her. How does he or she think the idea would work? Write everything down. You can help by offering your own thoughts but don't let it become just you doing this work. The client must be fully engaged. By being the recorder, you free the client up to do his or her own thinking.

Try to make each idea a possible solution. Get your client to think about how the idea would work. Look for ways to make the idea better than it first appeared. Make the idea, no matter how fantastical, as practical as possible. Link or merge an idea with another if it seems like the two compliment each other.

To get your client to do this exercise, say something like the following:

"So far, we've written down a bunch of ideas that are only thought fragments. We need to expand on these fragments to produce ideas that could be possible solutions. To do this, we'll expand ideas, make them bigger. We'll merge ideas that could work together. We'll think of all the ways an idea could be made to work. To do this, we have to follow a set of rules:

- No evaluation, censorship, or criticism of any idea.

- Do not pick a specific solution at this time.

- Elaborate and expand on all ideas.

- Merge ideas that are complimentary to each other.

- Clarify all ideas, allowing all thoughts about what the idea means to surface.

I suggest we use this elaboration sheet (*pointing at the IDEA, ELABORATION, CLARIFICATION sheet*) to make sure we do this with every idea."

One way to expand an idea is to take turns and guess at the many possible meanings of the idea. If both of you look for different possible meanings for a recorded idea, the idea grows and new ways of looking at the idea will emerge.

Record all guesses. You don't have to arrive at one meaning for the idea. Again, the more possibilities your client identifies as possible meanings, there is a better chance an optimum idea will suddenly emerge.

Hitchhiking is one useful technique for elaborating on ideas and amounts to saying, "This idea is a good one and it will take us even further if we add (*this and that*) to it." It's the process of thinking of ideas in terms of the idea plus any additions that might make it even better. Search for ways to improve what is already contained in the idea.

To elaborate on ideas, don't just list ideas. You can make them fleshed out visual ideas. Freehand draw them. This is akin to entrepreneurs at lunch drawing innovative ideas out on paper napkins. Allow your mind(s) to better understand ideas and to see new possibilities by visualizing them and drawing them out. Sketch without worrying about the quality of the drawing. Just illustrate the idea and any ways to enhance it.

Sometimes the quality of a given idea increases when we add it to another idea, even though that idea was generated as a separate possibility. The list of solution possibilities may have an idea that could match and complement another idea. The joined ideas might become a viable solution – "We could do this, this and this and get great results." By pooling what several ideas offer, your client may in fact identify an optimum solution.

SIMPLIFICATION OPTION: You can still do this step without the structure of the IDEA, ELABORATION, CLARIFICATION chart by teaching your client to first group ideas that seem similar, and then to think about how each idea could be made even better. You could say something like:

> "Bill, you've done a great job of coming up with ideas. I feel good about the work we've done so far. Now, the next step is to make sure we fully understand each idea and look for ways to make each idea even better. We have one main rule at this stage – no criticism of any idea. We're only looking to improve ideas right now. We can do this by grouping ideas together, and by adding to each idea to make it more likely to work. We'll start with the first idea on our list. Do you see any other ideas that could be added to it to make it a better idea?"

WHEN TO MOVE TO THE NEXT STAGE

It's time to move to the next step once both you and your client really know each idea, once all ideas have been clarified, and when your best efforts have been made to:

- elaborate and expand each idea,

- group ideas that compliment each other to create workable solutions,

143

and

- find all of the best attributes of each idea.

A decision as to which idea is the best solution should not yet have been made. Do not move forward until all ideas have been fully clarified, enhanced and turned as closely as they can be into fully developed ideas that could work.

TRANSITION TO THE NEXT STAGE

To move forward, you need to lead your client to the next step by saying something like,

> "We're now shifting to critical thinking. We have to put each solution to the test. We want to know if we can predict that it will overcome your constraints and achieve the desired outcomes, with the resources that we have available, within the deadline period you require?"

or

> "Things are moving forward really well. You've been quite creative in coming up with ideas and making them even better by elaborating them. Now, we're going to shift to critical thinking. We have to figure out which solution possibilities satisfy your decision criteria. When you defined the problem, you said your solution must overcome each of your constraints, meet your minimal expectations and produce the benefits of (_the client's E^3 outcomes_) by your deadline. Our next step is to evaluate each idea to see if it can do that."

STEP EIGHT:
EVALUATE EACH
SOLUTION OPTION

Up until now, you and your client suspended your critical thinking while focussing on more creative processes. It's now time to make a shift to more organized, structured, critical, judgmental, evaluative thinking. Together, you've generated many solution possibilities and you must now consider whether or not each possibility will deliver what is wanted and which of them are the best possible solutions.

Insight Potential When "Evaluating" – *By using structured processes to fairly evaluate each idea against the same criteria, an idea might emerge as a best possible solution when it may have originally been discarded. In turn, what might have first appeared as a workable solution might be discovered wanting in a key manner that means the solution can't produce the desired outcomes within the deadline. Surprises can result as the ideas are all compared against the same requirements. By treating all ideas in the same way, by evaluating all ideas against the same criteria, it's possible you and your client will surprise yourselves when you discover which idea produces the best benefits with the least cost of implementation.*

Hopefully, this step involves the first appearance of any critical thinking or negative assessment of the ideas that were generated as possible solutions. Everything should have been done to prevent such criticism and evaluation before this moment. Now, the two of you will evaluate each of the ideas.

GOALS OF EVALUATION

This step does not involve making a decision. It's the step to prepare for one, and the goals include:

- Fairly evaluate all ideas.

- Identify all of the strengths, advantages, and benefits of each idea <u>before</u> considering any negatives, weaknesses, and costs.

- Continue to expand on ideas by adding not yet considered elements that might surface during the evaluation phase.

- Compare all ideas with the same measures.

and,

- Use measures that match your primary decision criteria – what must each idea satisfy to be considered an optimum solution?

Put on your analytic hats and evaluate each of the ideas to get a measure of the potential payoffs, and then the costs of implementing each option. At this stage, each idea must now demonstrate that it's the best possible solution.

Once again, the actual selection of the solution to be implemented is delayed until a later step. A decision will be made, but not now.

RULES FOR EFFECTIVE EVALUATION

A few principles should shape your behavior at this stage. Many ideas are better than a few. Clarifying and expanding ideas is better than stressing over the righteousness of them. Looking for the positives about each idea first is better than "knocking all of the stuffing out of an idea then trying to find something good about it." Believing in the positive value of ideas is better than just being cynical. And lastly, all ideas should be measured against the same criteria.

Consequently, within this model, there are specific rules to be followed when the two of you evaluate all of the solution ideas.

- Agree on the evaluation criteria first.

- Look for the positives first, and then the negatives.

and,

- Record everything.

Ideas have a better chance of surviving this step if you look for what's good about an idea before you look for its weaknesses. By thinking about what makes an idea a good one, you retain a little bit of that creative thinking from the earlier steps. You'll find you can still identify ways to improve an idea before you criticize it.

All ideas are to be evaluated using the same criteria. The criteria should directly relate to the available resources, the constraints, intended outcomes (the client's E^3 results), and the required deadline. Decide, in advance, what criteria will be used to evaluate each of the ideas. All ideas should be treated equally. Get your client to understand this requirement by saying something like:

> "(*Name Of Your Client*), for this step, we're going to talk about what's good about each idea before we look at what's negative about the idea. Ultimately we're going to determine if each idea can be implemented with your available resources, overcome your constraints of (*list the constraints*), meet your minimal expectations of (*list the minimal expectations*), give you the desired benefits of (*list the desired E^3 benefits*), and work well enough to bring about these changes by your deadline of (*state the client's wished for date for the change to be made*). We need to work through the ideas methodically – positives first then what's not good enough about each idea, and as we do this, we need to make sure we think about each idea in terms of your decision criteria."

If possible, list your client's criteria on a large sheet of paper so they're front and center to the rest of the process of evaluating. The criteria are contained within the client's S.P.I.C.E^3. For example, the decision criteria might include cost relative to available resources, constraints (which might relate to what the client can afford), expected benefits, convenience, time requirements, resources required, impact on others, comfort, etc. Make sure your client agrees with the identified criteria, and accepts that only the identified criteria will be used. When finished with the evaluation of an idea, check to see if all criteria were applied to that idea before moving to the next.

In this step, there are several ways to organize your work. Pick an approach that seems to best fit the nature of your client's problem. Less difficult problems or those not considered to be high-payoff problems can use simple evaluation techniques that involve an assessment of the positives and negatives of each idea. More complex problems, or those seen as almost impossible to solve, or those where significant gains could be realized, should involve more deliberate and thorough evaluation processes.

A commonly used and simple evaluation technique is the Pro/Con approach. First think about the positive aspects of each idea. The entire focus would be on what's good. Interrupt or stop any thinking about what's wrong with an idea until you've both looked at each one in positive ways. One you've looked at all of the positive reasons each idea is a possible solution, then start with the first idea and identify the arguments against it. Move through all ideas considering the cons, keeping the decision criteria in mind as you do so.

Alternatively, you could use the payoff vs. costs approach. Make two lists for each idea. One will list the potential payoffs or gains to be achieved by using the idea. List as many of these potential gains as you can. A gain could be financial, emotional, relationship based, or other intangible results.

The second list will identify the costs associated with each idea. A cost could be any expenditure required to implement an idea, any negative impacts on any person or aspect of the problem situation, or any losses that might result. Expenditures could be measured in terms of emotion, effort, resources, or actual dollar costs that would be consumed to make the idea work.

Complete the payoffs list first because it is too easy to think of negatives and prematurely reject ideas because the payoffs weren't fairly considered. By thinking of positives first, each idea is more effectively considered. After the payoffs and costs have been considered for each idea, your client will have a better sense of which ideas have the best payoffs at the least cost.

Another way to evaluate ideas is to look into the future and guess at the consequences that might be experienced by implementing each idea. It's useful to make three lists of anticipated results. One list specifies the results to be experienced immediately upon implementation. The second list can focus on those short-term results that might be expected in the follow-up period after implementation. The third list is then used to identify those consequences that might be predicted over a longer period of time.

To make the lists, consider each idea and brainstorm what you and your client think might happen if it were implemented as the solution. Don't question, challenge, or criticize the guesses. Just think forward and anticipate both the benefits and what could go wrong once the solution has been implemented. Add your own thoughts to stimulate your client's thinking.

In most cases, you'll be able to use one of the approaches identified above. But when working on very difficult problems, where the costs of failure are too high, it's helpful to use a method that involves the building of a comprehensive matrix. A matrix is a graphic method of organizing and illustrating information. A matrix organizes as much information as possible about the values of each solution alternative.

Set up a matrix before any evaluation is done and then proceed to evaluate every idea within the matrix against all of the criteria in the matrix:

1. Across the top of your matrix, list the decision criteria your client will use to make a selection of a solution for this problem.

2. Down the left hand side of the matrix, list the expanded ideas.

3. Evaluate each alternative idea, as objectively as possible, against each of the criteria.

4. Looking at all of the information that has been filled in the boxes in the matrix, rank each idea based on how well each idea has satisfied all of the criteria.

The matrix evaluation procedure surfaces and makes public all of the information pertinent to evaluation. It treats all ideas equally in terms of time given to consideration and inhibits the premature formation of strong preferences. Some ideas emerge as the better choices on the basis of comparison of all ideas against the same criteria. The structure of the matrix emphasizes the priority of the decision criteria so ideas are seen as best for the right reasons.

Criteria

Solution Ideas	Essential			Desired			Optional				Overall Rank
	Cr #1	Cr #2	Cr #3	Cr #4	Cr #5	Cr #6	Cr #7	Cr #8	Cr #9	Cr #10	
A											
B											
C											
D											
E											
F											
G											
H											

Solution Ideas Are Written Out In Their
Clarified And Expanded Form

However, the matrix evaluation process takes considerable time to complete. Recording all of the information feels like a chore and can produce frustration with the focus on considering all details before making a decision.

It's possible to simplify and quantify the matrix by entering a rating in each square based on how your client sees an idea falling on each decision criteria. For example, if the idea is seen as exceptional in a given decision criteria, it would be assigned a 10, and conversely if the idea is seen as very weak, then a 0 or 1 could be assigned. By adding all of the ratings across the line for that idea, a supposed quantifiable result would be shown.

This is a very complex evaluation process that is likely to be most useful when dealing with very difficult or potentially high-payoff problems. It takes time to complete a full matrix especially when there are many solution ideas and many decision criteria to be considered. However, that's when the potential payoffs justify the work involved.

When the matrix is large, work on completion of the matrix over several sessions. It does not have to be done all in one sitting and makes the time spent more productive because there is less information fatigue. In turn, breaking the evaluation step into two or more sessions makes the completion of a complex matrix much more pleasurable.

SIMPLIFICATION OPTION: In those situations where you're working in an environment that precludes working with large sheets of paper, where you're working with an impatient client, or where you think the client's level of functioning requires use of the easiest technique, then use the pro/con approach. Most people have encountered this before and it's close to what we do naturally. When preparing for a decision, we often create mental lists for why we should decide one way and why we shouldn't. You'll still need to manage the structuring of this process but you can make it easier for your client by saying something like:

> "Jill, it's time to figure out which ideas are better than others. We have a list of possible solution ideas and we need to figure out why you should use each idea and why you shouldn't. To do this, we'll assess the pros and cons of each idea. We're not going to pick one just yet, but we're working in that direction by fairly considering each idea. So the first idea on our list is to (*state that idea*). What do you think are the reasons that this is a good idea?" (when required, add in your own thoughts to stimulate your client's thinking)

WHEN TO MOVE TO THE NEXT STEP

It's time to move to the next step when you've considered the positive values of each idea first, then identified the negative aspects of each idea, and organized this information in a readily reviewable format. Whichever technique you've used, you want your client to really understand the potential benefits for each idea and the potential negative consequences if an idea is implemented.

You can move forward when both of you know that:

- there are several solution ideas that will achieve the desired E^3 benefits and results,

- these ideas do not have any inherent downsides or negative costs your client doesn't want to experience, either now or later as time passes,

- your client can afford to implement these solutions,

- your client has the necessary resources to make each solution work (people, money, space, equipment, etc.) or has access to such resources,

- these different options will overcome any of the real constraints and roadblocks,

and

- your client has options that can be fully implemented by his or her deadline.

Don't move forward until all ideas have been fully considered. Your client should not have made any decisions yet or selected any particular solutions but this process of evaluating ideas should be getting your client significantly closer to doing so because that is the next step.

TRANSITION TO THE NEXT STEP

Upon recognizing that the evaluation step has been completed, you could say something like:

"Wow! We've identified several really good possibilities to choose from. It's time to make a decision."

or

"Okay, we've reached crunch time. We've comprehensively looked at each idea so now a decision must be made. Are we ready?"

or

"Every idea has been expanded, clarified and fairly evaluated with the intent of finding the optimum solution(s) to your problem. It's time now to make a decision so let's move to the next step. Are you okay with that?"

STEP NINE:
DECIDE
(PICK THE OPTIMUM SOLUTIONS)

> Your client should now have an abundance of real solution possibilities to consider. It's time for your client to select the best solution or combination of solutions that will yield the optimum results, bring about the desired change, all within the resources your client has available, and by the required deadline. The two of you will now go from a broad focus on all possibilities to a narrow focus on the best possible solutions.

Insight Potential When "Deciding" – *Your client may be surprised that a combination of solutions is possible and will yield the best outcomes. In turn, your client may be surprised by what he or she ultimately selects as the best solutions. Your client has the potential of selecting a solution he or she would not have considered before engaging in this process of creative problem-solving, but now sees as obviously the best solution.*

154

From all of the solution possibilities, invite your client to select those options that will best close the problem gap between where your client is now and where he or she wants to be.

GOALS OF THE DECISION STEP

The ultimate goal is to select a solution or set of solutions with the highest probability of resulting in the exciting benefits desired by your client. Ideally, you want your client to:

- identify the optimum solution(s) based on all of the information the two of you gathered and organized,

- select solutions that yield your client's desired E^3 outcomes, or if several solutions meet your client's criteria, then select those that give your client the greatest benefits beyond his or her desired E^3 outcomes,

- select only solutions that can be and will be successfully implemented before the deadline is reached,

- select only solutions that your client can afford to implement given available resources,

and

- select solutions that best overcome your client's constraints.

Your client should believe this is his or her decision to make, that the selection can be made of his or her own volition, and that he or she is selecting the right solution. Your client should believe the solution is one he or she can fully commit to, so the solution is effectively implemented.

> An idea that appears to be the best idea but won't be implemented well, or on time, is an inadequate solution.

Prior to making a selection, get your client to first decide on the decision-making method most appropriate for the given situation. The decision process may seem obvious if your client is only one person, however even an individual could decide whether to:

155

- sleep on the information and let his or her subconscious mind decide via a dream or sudden insight,

- act now on his or her own, and just decide,

- seek advice from a confidant,

- canvas several others for their preferences,

or

- decide, then invite others to challenge the decision and change his or her mind if feedback is constructive and critical.

Even as an individual, your client should clarify in his or her own mind how he or she is going to make the decision so the decision actually gets made.

> "(*Name Of Your Client*), It's time to make a decision. You have several options to choose from. You can make your decision now, wait and sleep on this before you decide, or talk to others to get their opinion. Do you feel ready to decide?"

Sometimes it pays to sleep on all of the information that has been organized in the preceding steps. The greatest part of human information processing occurs outside of conscious awareness. This information will percolate subconsciously as your client does other things. Input from the subconscious mind can come in very indirect and roundabout ways. Allow the final selection to arise from clues presented in dreams, or how your client's attention wanders, or what your client suddenly becomes more aware of in his or her surroundings.

Often it's a "gut decision" that takes us in the right direction. Doing the full evaluation of each idea makes this possible. All that information is now available to our subconscious processes, and below our awareness we may be making a decision. By deliberately attending to clues from the subconscious process, your client's effectiveness at the selection step in problem-solving will improve.

Encourage your client to make a choice that includes more than one solution possibility. This package of solutions can include ideas that complement each other, extend each other, or cover different targets. This package may contain ideas to be implemented all at once, or ideas to be initiated in sequence according to a previously specified order, or the package might contain back-up or contingency ideas to be implemented should the first selected idea fail.

In some selection situations, your client may find him or her self stuck trying to choose between two equally desirable alternatives. The first thing to do is to determine if, in fact, it's necessary to choose between them. Perhaps you're client is free to choose both and not have to exclude one in favor of the other. Sometimes the simple decision is to select both to be implemented together, separately or in sequence.

However, there are times when limited resources require a decision between two equally desirable solutions. You can suggest different methods to determine if your client truly does regard the two options as equal.

- let someone else decide (that could be you),

- flip a coin,

or

- pick one and wait.

As soon as one of these has been done, does your client immediately realize that he or she wishes a different result had emerged? Conversely, does your client experience a sense of relief and a feeling of gladness that the choice has been made? Either way, from your client's reaction, both of you will know your client's own true selection.

CHOOSE THE OPTIMUM SOLUTION(S)

Your client should select the idea or a set of ideas with the greatest potential of achieving the full set of E^3 benefits within your client's deadline, at a cost your client can afford, while overcoming your client's real constraints. Upon making that selection, your client should feel some excitement about getting this new solution into action.

If that enthusiasm is missing, it's likely that an optimum solution has not been selected. It's not enough to decide to do something that only feels adequate or acceptable. The solution or solutions should feel exciting because the solution will deliver the desired benefits and results, overcome any constraints, and be implemented within the deadline.

If your client doesn't have what he or she believes is the best solution, then back up to the beginning and go through the process again; or back-up to the "Generating Solutions" Step and brainstorm additional ideas; or back up to the "Elaborate and Clarify" step and work harder on clarifying and expanding the creative ideas into workable solutions; or back-up and re-evaluate any ideas that might have been prematurely rejected.

You need to get your client to decide. The client could elect to make the decision later but you want to then schedule a next appointment to discuss what he or she has decided because you still aren't done. It's your responsibility to get your client to make a selection.

SIMPLIFICATION OPTION: This step is already pretty straightforward. Your task is to direct your client to select one or more of the options to be implemented. You can say something as simple as:

> "Bill, which of these alternatives looks best to you? What do you want to do to solve this problem?"

WHEN TO MOVE TO THE NEXT STEP

You're ready to move to the next step when a clear decision has been made, and your client feels some degree of enthusiasm about getting the solution put into place. You can proceed when your client has locked on to a solution or set of solutions you believe will close the problem gap and your client could successfully implement by the deadline.

TRANSITION TO THE NEXT STEP

Review what your client has decided, then congratulate your client on making a decision. Then indicate it's now time to develop a plan for getting the solution implemented. You could say something like,

"Okay, You've chosen what you believe is the best solution. Well done. Now we need to figure out just exactly how you're going to implement it."

You could also stipulate that it's now time to specify who will do what, when, how, where, and with what resources.

"This is great. You've made a decision and you now have a strong expectation you will get the results you want. It's my understanding   you've decided to (_whatever the client has decided to do_). However, to make sure this happens, we need to make a plan for how you'll implement this solution. We aren't done yet. You need to decide when and where you will do this, how, and with what resources."

PART THREE – GETTING THE CLIENT TO "ACT"

You've helped your client identify a solution or set of solutions to his or her problem but more has to be done to get this problem fully resolved. It's time to plan for how the solution will be implemented, put the solution into play, then assess whether or not the solution has produced the desired E^3 benefits and outcomes.

STEP TEN:
ACTION PLANNING

The problem has not yet been solved. Your client's chosen solution(s) must first be put into action. However, before that happens, the two of you should plan out how each solution, and each aspect of each solution, is to be implemented. Clearly specify who will do what, when, where, how, with what resources, and why. Without this clarity, the solution will likely not be properly executed, and hence fail. By developing a thorough action plan, you help your client to prevent failure and increase the chances of successful resolution of his or her problem.

Insight Potential When "Action Planning" – *Your client may discover the details that make a difference between the solution working and not working. By developing the action plan, fundamental weaknesses of the solution might be revealed, thereby preventing implementation of a solution that will only fail. On the other hand, your client may determine that implementation will be easier than he or she had worried would be the case.*

Once your client has arrived at a solution or set of solutions, the two of you must clarify how this solution will be put into action. It must be clearly specified who will do what, when, where, how, using what resources, and why. In addition, by reinforcing the why of each action to be taken, your client doesn't lose sight of what he or she is working to achieve.

GOALS OF ACTION PLANNING

This step precedes the actual implementation of a solution. The primary objective at this step is to get ready. There are several goals for this step:

- Clearly build an action plan in which the full sequence of action steps are defined and arranged in the optimum order.

- Make sure your client is aware of what he or she has to do to put the solution(s) into effect.

- Uncover and resolve any differences in understanding about just how the solution is to work.

and

- Build confidence the solution can be effectively implemented and will work.

THE ELEMENTS OF AN ACTION PLAN

There are many details that affect the implementation of any solution. This step allows your client to address each of the details that matter. Action planning requires clarity in seven different dimensions:

What	What are the specific actions to be done?
Who	Who is going to do each action?
With What Resources	What resources are needed to complete each action?
Where	Where is each action going to occur and where are the resources needed to complete the action located?

When	When is each action going to occur, and how does one know it's time for each action (the signal for each action to start)? Identify checkpoints to stop and ensure the plan is working.
How	How specifically will each action be done (specific steps and behaviors)?
Why	Why each action must occur? Answering why the client is doing this reminds him or her of the desired E^3 results, the constraints that must be overcome, and the desired deadline.

Work to make sure your client's plan has specific details for each of these seven dimensions. Be as specific and as clear as possible so there is little room for misunderstanding. Your client in particular, and each other person involved in the implementation of this new solution, should know exactly what is expected of him or her, and when he or she is to act.

To begin this step, explain to your client it's now time to make an action plan so the solution is implemented properly.

"(*Name Of Your Client*), before you actually put your solution into effect, we need to sort out exactly how you're going to do that. We need to make a plan of action. This requires being very specific about who will do what, where, when, how, with what resources, and why. The "who" is mostly you, but given that you might need help accessing certain resources, I probably have a role to play as well. We need to sort out what each of us will do. So are you ready to sort this out?"

Write out the plan of action. By externalizing the plan and making it visible for scrutiny, it's much easier to detect missing aspects of the plan. As well, this written record serves as a stimulant for more complete thinking about all aspects of the plan. Most importantly, this written record serves as a reference point later in the implementation step.

In order for a plan to work, and to increase the probability the plan will be carried out, your client needs to be very specific in his or her plans. Get your client to use descriptive terms rather than general terms. There should be no confusion that trips your client up and then causes delays or any failure that prevents the solution from working.

The plan should also be very specific about the timing of the specific behaviors. Specify exactly when each behavior should happen. Identify the signals or cues that should be present to indicate the behavior is now appropriate. A solution that isn't implemented in a clear and sequential fashion isn't likely to succeed. The plan needs to make sure your client does his or her part when called for, so the sequence stays intact.

For example:

GENERAL
I'll go back to school to complete my high school diploma requirements.

SPECIFIC
When I leave here, I'll use one of the bus chits you said your secretary will give me and go to the Public School Administration Building on Hill Street to ask how I can get admission to complete my high school diploma. I'll inquire about any special programs for people my age who wish to return to school.

Once I have the information, I'll complete all forms for admission. You said you would write a letter of recommendation for me to support that application. I'll let you know if and when I need that letter, then you could write it and I will pick it up.

If I need to pay for these studies, I'll call my parents and ask if I can come for Tuesday dinner to discuss my plans. Then at dinner, I'll ask my dad, who said he would pay for my education if I ever decided to go back, for financial support.

I need to get off the streets so I'm first going to approach Hope Mission, explain what I'm trying to do, and ask if they

164

can provide any support, particularly in terms of a place to live. If they're unable to do so, I'll ask my parents if I can move back home to allow me to return to school and complete my high school program.

I hope to have all of this done by our appointment on Friday of next week. I'm going to do all of this to get my high school diploma so I can then apply for the plumbing apprenticeship program through NAIT.

One bit of failure is all it will take to cause your client to resort back to his or her status quo behaviors. The more specific the plan is, the better the chance of successful implementation. Essentially, your client's plan can't be too detailed. Your client's success is directly related to an effective execution of a detailed plan of action.

It's very important to specify the implementation period. By setting a time when the implementation is to start and a time by which the implementation period is to be complete, your client can work toward this deadline. This deadline gives urgency to the successful completion of all of the tasks.

In some cases, a solution will result in failure if not completed on time. By being clear about the implementation period, your client knows this is a critical component of success and will work more urgently toward complete implementation. Your client should know and understand the importance of both the start and end dates.

After your client thinks he or she has completed a full action plan, it's helpful to read or review the plan to ensure the plan clearly indicates all seven important dimensions. Read the plan looking for detail and find the aspects of the plan that specify:

- who
- will do what
- when
- where
- how
- with what resources
- and why.

Review the plan and place a check mark on the list as you determine that each element has been covered. This makes sure all the important dimensions to action planning are covered before implementation is initiated. If something is missing, implementation will break down, leading your client to see the solution as a failure and resort back to the status quo.

Some problems only require very simple action plans because the solutions are brief one or two act events. In such cases, it's enough for your client to make a quick summary statement which answers the seven basic questions – "Who is going to do what, where, when, how, with what resources, and why?" Even though the answers to a given problem situation may appear obvious, it's extremely useful to verbalize and record them.

For some problem situations, it might be enough to have your client make a personal commitment list that contains all the things your client will do in the order in which he or she will do them. The last item in the list should summarize the E^3 outcome that your client has determined he or she wants to achieve by solving the problem.

By writing out this series of tasks as personal commitment statements, your client has a checklist to hold him or herself responsible for completing the tasks as and when they should be completed:

- I will…
- Then I will...
- Then I will…
- Because I want…

This is a variation of the "To Do" list. By writing each task as a commitment statement, your client is making a clear declaration that he or she will follow-through with the complete implementation. Such commitments can be very useful because the draw to return to the status quo is very strong. By closing with a clear statement of the desired benefits to be achieved by implementing the solution, your client reminds him or herself why these tasks must be done successfully.

SIMPLIFICATION OPTION: For action planning to be effective, the seven questions must be asked. However, instead of adding the structure of writing the answers out on large visible sheets, you could walk the client through the series of questions and write down the answer to each question on a notepad. You want to encourage your client to be as specific as possible about each answer.

For example, you could say something like:

> "Bill, you've made your decision but before you leave to implement it, I think we should do a little planning to make sure the solution works. I want you to succeed and your chances of doing so will go up if we answer a few questions first. I want you to be as specific as possible about exactly what's going to happen.
>
> What exactly are you going to do?
>
> Who else will be involved – do you need anyone else there or available to help in any way?
>
> What resources do you need to have available so you can do what you're going to do?
>
> Tell me exactly how you're going to do this?
>
> Where are you going to do each action?
>
> When are you going to do this and when can I check to see that things are proceeding as planned?
>
> Now, remind me why you're doing this? What are you trying to achieve?
>
> Looks like a good plan. I'm proud of you for doing this. I want to know how it's going for you as you do this so I can congratulate you along the way. I'll call as planned."

WHEN TO MOVE TO THE NEXT STEP

You'll know you're both ready to proceed to the next step where the solution will actually be implemented when you have:

- specified clearly who is going to do what, where, when, how, with what resources, and why,

- specified what is to be the trigger that indicates implementation can begin,

- specified the order in which everything is to take place,

- prescribed the checkpoints by which your client will be able to recognize whether or not the action plan is operating as it should,

and

- prepared a written record of the plan for easy visual reference.

When you've satisfied the above criteria, you're ready for implementation.

TRANSITION TO THE NEXT STEP

You've done your work helping your client get to the point where a solution has been picked and an action plan worked out. You need to hand responsibility for carrying out that solution over to your client:

"(*Name Of Your Client*), you now know what can be done to solve this problem. You have a solution and a plan for putting it into action. It's now up to you. I want to meet with you again after you've put the solution into effect so we can assess how well it's working. Let's meet in three weeks on the same day and at the same time. Meanwhile, I'll call on the days we specified in the plan. I'm looking forward to seeing what you accomplish."

STEP ELEVEN:
CHANGE
(IMPLEMENTATION OF THE SOLUTION)

To solve the problem, to bring about successful change, the plan must be put into action and the solution implemented. In the process of executing the solution, there are still some things you and your client can do to minimize the costs of any failure and increase the chance of success. Ideally, this would have been decided in the action planning step.

Insight Potential When "Changing" – *Your client may discover the solution works as intended, or alternatively that the solution fails to generate the desired results within the deadline, or the results might far exceed expectations. Your client might discover certain details were not satisfactorily addressed in the action plan and changes need to be made so the solution can be implemented properly; or your client might discover this solution works but introduces some new problems that have to be resolved.*

Your client has reached this stage because he or she felt the need to bring about some sort of change and sought a counseling session with you. You then helped your client to define his or her S.P.I.C.E^3, and you taught some basic problem-solving principles so your client could work with you to solve his or her own problem. Together, you brainstormed a large number of solution possibilities, sought to better know each idea by elaborating and clarifying each option, and evaluated them by looking for the best aspects of each idea before considering weaknesses. Your client then made a decision – a selection of a solution or a package of solutions that would predictably achieve the client's desired E^3 outcomes. Then, together you mapped out a sufficiently comprehensive implementation plan. Now, it's time to get your client's problem solved and bring about effective change.

GOALS OF THIS STEP

The most significant goals of this step in the change process are to:

- Fully implement the plan.

- Prevent failure or reduce the costs of failure to the lowest possible level.

- Increase the chances of success.

- Measure progress along the way toward full implementation.

- Make adjustments if the encounter with reality means the implementation plan is breaking down.

- Achieve the specified E^3 outcomes, thereby solving your client's problem.

- Meet any deadlines for full implementation.

and

- Have your client feel significant satisfaction with the change process and the changes he or she accomplishes.

A successful implementation will achieve all of these goals. If so, the client's problem(s) will be solved thereby creating a new status quo in which the payoffs and benefits exceed what was being achieved in the old one.

TECHNIQUES FOR EFFECTIVE IMPLEMENTATION

There are various things you and your client can do to insure effective change. Care must be taken to ensure the solution is truly applied as it was intended to be and it's not breaking down during the implementation step.

Get your client to track progress with particular consideration for whether or not everything is progressing on time, and whether or not each of the activities produces the necessary outcomes. You can check on progress by contacting your client when you know significant actions should have just been completed. Ask how everything is going and congratulate your client for each successful action.

In some cases, you might call and find your client has doubts about the effectiveness of the solution. Tell your client to look for weaknesses in the action plan that can be corrected before it's too late. Get your client to fix any issues so the ultimate deadline can be met.

By monitoring progress at each of the checkpoints, your client can determine if the plan is working as intended. Monitoring could show that the implementation plan is working flawlessly and your client can be reassured the right plan is in place. If a well-developed action plan is monitored during implementation and is discovered to not be working as intended, your client must stop, adjust, and make a new plan. Fix the points where the plan is breaking down and monitor for improvement.

However, in some situations, by monitoring progress, it may become evident to you and your client that the solution is not solving the problem. In such an instance, you both must acknowledge the need to choose a new solution alternative. Backed by the surety the solution was implemented as intended, your client can let go of that particular solution when confronted with evidence it's not working.

Setting time limits for each stage of implementation and building in checkpoints reduces the likelihood of failure. However, if a well-developed plan has been followed, and the solution does not achieve the goals, then your client will be able to acknowledge the need to stop, back up and choose a new solution.

It's often possible, and wise, to set up safe, low risk, manageable trials of the solutions or solution package. It's not necessary to always risk everything on a full implementation. Full implementation takes on the risk of dramatic change before fully knowing if the solution will actually work and actually achieve the E^3 outcomes.

A trial provides a good opportunity for rehearsal and fine-tuning. Confidence is built up before taking on the full problem situation. If a trial is conducted first, any weaknesses in either the implementation plan or the solution will be discovered before the full costs of failure occur.

A trial run can make the change process more tolerable because we know we can revert back to the old status quo if the new solution doesn't produce the desired E^3 outcomes, or at least outcomes better than the old status quo. Plus, when everything works as intended, a much more positive expectation the solution will work is fostered.

There are different methods for trial implementation. One common method is to identify an example of the real problem situation and try the solution out only on that smaller sample. For example, the solution could be tried out with family before attempting to implement it at work. If the solution doesn't work there, then corrective action must be taken before attempting to deal with a riskier context.

In some problem situations, particularly those involving interpersonal interaction, it's possible to conduct a role-play using the new solution. This allows your client to explore how he or she would respond to the reactions of others in the role-play. Each participant in the role-play could then share how the solution felt to him or her. Such feedback may trigger minor adjustments to the action plan or to the solution itself, or may demonstrate early on that the solution is not going to deliver the desired E^3 outcomes.

Such role-plays could involve you and your client, or perhaps someone else from your work place and your client. Your client could do what he or she is planning to do with this other person and receive feedback about its impact. If the feedback suggests a need to tweak the action plan, your client can safely do this. On the other hand, the experience might show the client the selected solution is not going to work and you will need to work with your client to make a different decision and a new action plan.

At some point, the real implementation must occur. If the client has a plan, has tested that plan through some sort of trial and found it works, then the solution must be put into place in the real life situation according to that plan. Support your client as he or she does so.

SIMPLIFICATION OPTION: The only thing I can suggest as a way to make the implementation process easier is to have your client put the selected solution into action in a safer environment. Do this whenever possible.

"Bill, let's try that action plan out right here in my office. I'm going to ask my secretary to come in and I'll explain your situation to her and she could role play your wife. I'll coach her on how you think your wife might respond. You could then put your plan into action with her right now, saying what you want to say to your wife and she'll respond as she thinks your wife might respond. That way, we can see if this will work the way you want it to. Sound okay?"

WHEN TO MOVE TO THE NEXT STEP

Yes, there is a next step even after the solution has been fully implemented. You're ready to move to the next step when your client has:

- followed the full action plan and implemented the complete solution or solution package,

- implemented the solution before the deadline,

or

- the action plan has broken down.

When the above criteria have been met, you're ready to conduct a follow-up assessment of your client's results and problem-solving effort.

TRANSITION TO THE NEXT STEP

There is a learning opportunity here that you and your client should take advantage of. You're going to tally the results your client has achieved. This next step is deliberately part of the "GET STOKED & ACT" counseling approach. Because you know the specific date the solution will be put into action and the date by which results will be evident, schedule a meeting with your client to do a tally:

"Okay, once you've fully implemented your solution, we need to get together and study both the results you achieved, and how well you did as a problem-solver. When we meet, I'll ask you, "Did your solution achieve your E^3 goals, exceed them, or fall short?" and, "Did we work through the problem-solving sequence as well as we could have?" Your plan calls for your solution to be in full effect within three weeks. Can we meet three weeks from today at the same time? "

STEP TWELVE:
TALLY THE RESULTS
(ASSESS)

You want to make sure your client achieved the intended results. You also want your client to learn from this particular experience. Measure the results your client achieved and examine the process the two of you followed to get to that solution. Determine if the desired E^3 outcome has been achieved. Quantify what was accomplished. Then, work out why the results turned out as they did. Use hind-sight and review the problem-solving process the two of you followed. Look at how you did each step. If your client didn't get the intended results, try to establish where your shared problem-solving efforts came up short. Determine if anything could have been done more effectively. If your client achieved what he or she intended, or even more than your client intended, try to ascertain where your client was particularly effective so he or she can repeat that in future problem-solving situations. Then assess your own performance as a counselor.

Insight Potential When "Tallying" – *In examining the results achieved by your client's solution, the two of you may discover your client achieved what was intended, fell short, or exceeded his or her hoped for results. In turn, in looking at how your client worked on the problem, the two of you might discover weaknesses or new strengths in your client's problem-solving behavior. Recognizing what works can help your client to approach any new problems on his or her own. You might learn from your client's feedback.*

After the solution has been put into action, your client needs to determine if the solution accomplished what was intended. In addition, this is an important opportunity for your client to assess how much he or she learned about effective problem-solving. Lastly, this is your opportunity to learn more about how effective you have been in this counseling process.

GOALS OF THE TALLY STEP

It's now time to tally the results and assess what your client accomplished. Establish whether or not your client:

- arrived at the best possible solution(s),

- effectively used the problem-solving process,

- achieved personal satisfaction during this problem-solving event,

- enriched him or herself by effectively growing and developing both because of the solutions your client found and the process you guided your client through,

and

- enjoyed him or herself.

In addition, you want to establish what you did well and what could have been done differently to be more helpful to your client.

If your client ended with anything less, then you have a definite learning opportunity by identifying where the two of you came up short. If your client achieved all that could have been achieved, then your client can enter into his or her next problem-solving efforts with confidence. Your client now knows what he or she is doing as a creative, insight-oriented problem-solver.

This follow-up assessment addresses the quality of the solution and the quality of the process. The solution has to work and your client has to feel okay about how the solution was arrived at and implemented. In addition, assess how well you did during the counseling process. Did you help your client to achieve greater success? Did your client learn new skills and achieve greater independence? Did you follow the "GET STOKED & ACT" sequence as well as you could have?

ONGOING ASSESSMENT

Well before you reach the "Tally" step, it's your responsibility as a counselor to continuously assess your shared progress through the problem-solving process you're teaching your client to use. As you work with your client, continuously ask, "How are we doing as we do this step?" and, "Do we feel okay about what we're doing?" Any weaknesses can be identified and corrective coaching can be instituted along the way so the process improves and the final outcome is optimum.

Pay attention to the quality of the information you gather together, your process of gathering and organizing the information, and the degree of enjoyment and satisfaction you both have as the work is being done. Periodically check to see if your client is satisfied with the process and your progress.

Each time a particular problem-solving step is completed, ask your client how he or she feels about the quality of the work you did on that step. For example, you could ask, "Did we uncover all of the important information for this step of the problem-solving process?" or, "Did we work well together and bring out all of the important information that was needed at this stage?

By stopping for a few moments to assess how everything is proceeding, any necessary corrective action can be taken early in the process. By checking how your client feels about the problem-solving activity, it may be affirmed that everything is okay and the two of you can proceed with confidence.

FOLLOW-UP ASSESSMENT

Whether or not you conduct your follow-up assessment at the end of each problem-solving step, or at the end of having implemented the full solution, you need to do follow-up assessment. Earlier is better because you can make corrections as you're doing the work. However, you need to do a follow-up assessment for sure. Minimally, you and your client need to evaluate after the solution has been implemented to measure the results.

You may simply wish to assess by asking your client a set of diagnostic questions:

- Did we solve this problem and implement the solution in time?

- Did you achieve the desired E^3 outcomes (the minimal expectations, the exciting results and benefits you wanted to achieve, and within the time period by which you wanted to accomplish the change)?

- Did you utilize all available information and resources?

- Did you feel a high degree of confidence in your decision before the actual implementation of the solution?

- Did you enjoy the process of problem-solving?

- Did you learn anything as you problem-solved (any new insights about your problem, yourself, the skills, and the process of problem-solving)?

Through your client's answers to these questions, you'll know whether or not your client achieved the desired results and learned how to be a more effective problem-solver on his or her own.

The intention is to quantify as much as possible what your client really did achieve. Get very specific. Measure any financial gains. Try to quantify any emotional benefits the client realized. Make sure your client compares the old status quo to the new one and reinforce the benefits of this change.

Applaud your client for what he or she achieved. Then applaud how he or she did this. Review how the problem was solved. Remind your client of the steps he or she went through. Pat him or her on the back for taking effective action to bring about change.

This is the last step in the "GET STOKED & ACT" counseling approach and the last step in the problem-solving process. Make sure your client understands this. Teach the importance of assessing results after each implementation is complete. Point at the chart showing the problem-solving steps and make it clear your client should do this each time he or she solves another problem.

Then tell your client you want to assess how well your counseling has worked for him or her. Ask your client some finishing questions that focus on the ending of this counseling relationship?

- You had some apprehensions about coming to see a counselor. How has this process felt to you?

- Do you think this work we've done together has led to successful improvement in your situation?

- In this work together, did you learn new problem-solving skills you think you can apply on your own with future problems?

- How confident do you feel about being able to solve new problems using what you learned here?

- Is there anything you think I could have or should have done more effectively to be helpful to you?

You ask such questions to learn about your own performance in this counseling relationship. What did you do well? What could be improved so you're more effective next time? Get feedback from your client so you can be more helpful with future clients.

Once you've assessed how well the counseling sessions have gone, it's time to make it clear your counseling relationship is finished. You want to do this with compassion and grace, recognizing that through success, you've become important to the client's sense of well-being.

Separating after successful counseling can be tough for the client, especially if he or she thinks the successful change only came about because of you. You need to close with a summary of what the client did to achieve success.

Thank your client for the opportunity to work with him or her, and wish him or her well. Congratulate your client for what he or she achieved, and encourage your client to continue to use what he or she learned in your sessions to solve future problems on his or her own. You can offer to be a problem-solving resource if he or she encounters a particularly tough problem in the future, but re-affirm your faith that your client can now deal with most situations.

One of the counseling goals is to arrive at a point where your client is both more successful and able to independently continue to cope on his or her own. It's time to let that happen. Say goodbye with caring and encouragement.

SIMPLIFICATION OPTION: Again, it's tough to make this step any simpler than what I've just described, but I offer an example of what you can say:

> "Bill, now that you've applied your solution, did you get the results you wanted, and if so, please tell me what you've gained over what you had before?"
>
> "Great Bill, as you think about how we worked on your problem, how do you feel about this problem-solving process (_pointing at a sheet showing the problem-solving steps_)?"
>
> "Lastly Bill, I want your feedback on how I did as your counselor. How do you feel about how I worked with you? Is there anything you wish I had done differently?"

WHEN FINISHED

You'll know you've completed the "GET STOKED & ACT" counseling process when your client has:

- solved the problem by achieving his or her desired E^3 outcomes,
- measured and examined the quality of the results achieved,
- assessed the quality of his or her way of getting to this result,
- identified any existing strengths and weaknesses in his or her problem-solving behavior,

and

- taken credit for what he or she has done.

If, on the other hand, the results you've both achieved are not working out, you will need to transition back into the problem-solving steps.

TRANSITION BACKWARDS

Determine where your problem-solving process broke down and return to that step. If the problem was not properly defined, go right back to clarifying your client's S.P.I.C.E^3. The attempted solution may have revealed that a key aspect of the problem definition was missing.

"Bill, I think this indicates we didn't fully define the problem. We missed some of the constraints, and we failed to fully understand what was causing your difficulties. I want to re-visit your S.P.I.C.E^3 with you. Is that okay?"

Alternatively, it may be that the two of you didn't get creative enough in the brainstorming step and you'll need to look for other options. You could say something like:

"Bill, I think this solution just wasn't creative enough to solve your tough problem. I think we need to go back and generate some new possibilities using the brainstorming rules. No evaluation. Think of weird and far out ideas. Generate as many as we can. You okay with that?"

It may be that you weeded out other ideas before they were elaborated. It would be time to suggest bringing them back into focus and doing the elaboration step with them. You could say:

"Bill, the solution we picked didn't work and I think we need to revisit some of the creative ideas you generated earlier that we didn't elaborate on. Are you okay if we pull those ideas out and see if we can turn them into workable possibilities?"

You might have to revisit the evaluation step or even the decision step. Direct your client to the step you think needs to be revisited. Do this until the "GET STOKED & ACT process is truly completed.

The "GET STOKED & ACT" counseling process will be complete only when:

- your client is achieving greater success and a new status quo with better results and benefits,

- your client has expressed some degree of confidence in using new skills on future problems,

- you've received feedback about your contribution during the counseling process,

- you've assessed how well you followed the "GET STOKED & ACT" sequence of counseling steps,

and

- you've each said goodbye to acknowledge the end of this relationship.

CAUTIONS AND TIPS
(BE AS EFFECTIVE AS POSSIBLE)

There are subtle aspects of the counseling relationship that require your attention. You need to be cautious about the process of transference and dependence; about bumping up against your own ability to accept client feelings; and about using communication behaviors that get in the way of empathy and rapport. You need to particularly guard yourself against trying to solve your client's problem instead of holding the client responsible for engaging in the problem-solving process with you. You can also enhance your counseling performance by using the active listening skills and the problem-solving steps more frequently in your own relationships and work with colleagues. Lastly, look to take better care of yourself by letting go of your client's burdens and talking with a mentor about your counseling work.

Insight Potential By Attending To These Cautions and Tips – You might discover you're promoting your client's dependence on you because of some need to have others look to you as their hero. Perhaps, it will become evident you've taken on responsibility for your client's problem and feel pressure to come up with the right solution. You might discover your own behavior is keeping your client from opening up with you. Possibly, you'll notice you shy away from your client's intense feelings because of your own discomfort. You might also discover that the skills you're using would enhance your own personal relationships with family, friends and co-workers.

TRANSFERENCE AND DEPENDENCE

In any counseling relationship, transference can occur. Transference is a subconscious process. One person projects unresolved feelings, wishes, desires, expectations and beliefs that originated in prior relationships, onto the other person and contaminate the present. These prior relationships were usually primary kinships such as those of parent to child, sibling to sibling, or loved one to loved one.

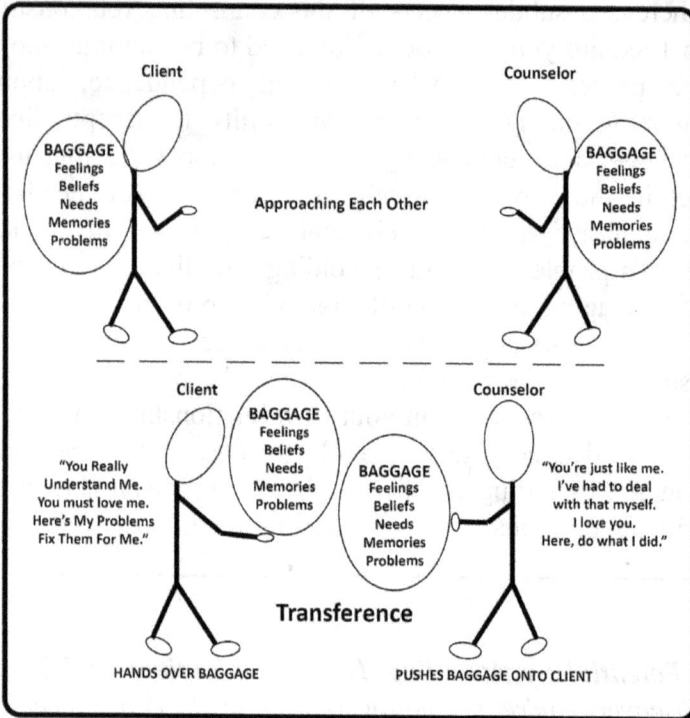

In other words, one person, without awareness of doing so, comes to see and relate to the other person as if the other person is a parent, child, sibling or loved one from his or her own past. Transference is about transferring some of the old feelings, positive or negative, of that prior relationship onto this other person in the present. Instead of being seen and heard clearly as him or herself, the other person is experienced as some clouded version distorted by the prior experiences, beliefs, feelings, and unfulfilled needs.

The risk of transference is particularly higher when one person offers empathy, compassion, full understanding, respect, and positive regard to another. It's highly likely your client has never experienced such treatment and has never felt so understood and respected. This process can be very intimate and thereby contains the risk one or both parties will experience affection, attachment, infatuation, idolatry, or love toward the other. This challenges the relationship you're building with your client and is not a healthy element in a helping relationship.

Transference and dependence can occur in two different directions – from the client to you, or more dangerously, from you to the client.

TRANSFERENCE FROM YOUR CLIENT TO YOU

If the client feels dependence, undue affection, misdirected anger, a need to please, subservience, or a desperate need to be told what to do, then transference has occurred. If the client feels like a child needing something from an important other, then transference has occurred.

The client might see you as so accepting, loving and competent that he or she will attempt to attach him or herself to you like a remora attaches to a shark, and hand over the problem(s) that brought him or her to you. Such a client could expect you to take responsibility for getting the problem solved, shifting into a passive mode and waiting to be told what you think he or she should do. By handing over responsibility for the problem, the client doesn't have to learn how to solve it on his or her own. The client becomes dependent on you for a solution.

The client may develop great feelings of appreciation, affection, infatuation, and possibly even love, making you a supremely valuable person to the client. The client might slip into seeing you as the parent the client wishes he or she had had as a child.

TRANSFERENCE FROM YOU TO YOUR CLIENT

If the counselor takes on any of the feelings the client has in his or her problem situation, such as frustration, hopelessness, despair, feeling stuck, loneliness, anger, or fear, then transference has occurred. If the counselor starts to feel parental toward the client, then transference has occurred. If the counselor thinks it's his or her responsibility to fix the client, transference has occurred. If you take on responsibility for getting the problem solved or if you want to make the client's life easier by offering advice, then you've succumbed to transference. If the counselor comes to experience inappropriate affection for the client, transference has occurred.

As a counselor, you have to be careful you don't start relating to your client as if he or she is a child, parent, sibling, or loved one from your past. This can be reflected in wanting to tell your client what to do, or wanting to protect your client from his or her problems, or harboring inappropriate feelings toward your client.

In addition, if you've personally had to deal with the same issues experienced by the client, you also have to avoid the assumption he or she is just like you and should do what you did. All too often, a counselor that succumbs to such transference will try to push his or her solution onto the client. This will usually trigger resistance in the client who knows at some level he or she is not the same as the counselor.

Another danger is coming to need the client's infatuation with both you and what you have to offer. If you find yourself wanting to be the expert, the compassionate counselor, the problem-solver that finds a solution for his or her clients, then you're developing a dependency on your clients. You need your clients to need you so you can achieve fulfillment from your work. That puts a heavy burden on the client and interferes with the client learning to be more self-sufficient.

DEALING WITH TRANSFERENCE

There are several steps you can follow to prevent and deal with transference.

- Assume there is a shared risk, police yourself so you avoid transferring your baggage to your clients, and make sure you don't take on responsibility for the client's issues.

    o Notice any client non-verbal clues that might suggest he or she is feeling any dependence, affection, or inappropriate feelings given the nature of the relationship you share, and use the feelings checking skill to find out if you're reading your client's emotions correctly.

- Notice any change in yourself that suggests you feel affection, responsibility, helplessness, or parental responsibility toward your client, and then remind yourself your purpose is to help clarify the client's problems, to teach effective problem-solving, and to guide the problem-solving behavior of your client so he or she finds the optimum solution.

• Use the structure of the "GET STOKED & ACT" approach to keep the relationship focused on the business of counseling.

• Humbly accept any messages of appreciation directed to you by your client, and then re-direct that appreciation by commenting on how well the client is doing at clarifying his or her problem (his or her S.P.I.C.E³), thinking creatively and coming up with many solution possibilities, clarifying his or her thinking before prematurely rejecting ideas, evaluating ideas against the same criteria, making a decision to which he or she can commit, and making an effective plan of action to implement the chosen solution.

• Periodically check with your client to see if he or she is feeling any increase in his or her confidence about solving the problem, then congratulate the client for any progress that is made.

• In general, avoid the following behaviors:

  - Any intimate physical contact between you, and most certainly any conduct others would describe as inappropriate.

  - Exchanging personal information for how you can connect with each other outside of counseling sessions.

  - Allowing the client to praise you for solving his or her problem(s).

  - Accepting a request from the client to do something he or she should do personally.

  - Giving gifts to your client or accepting them in turn.

187

Keep effective personal boundaries between the two of you in your counseling relationship. The relationship is about helping your client to find ways to solve his or her own problems, and nothing more. It is not a friendship or anything more involving than the relationship you share in the counseling environment.

If either of you drifts over the other person's boundaries, comment on and challenge the behavior. If your client attempts to cross your boundaries and make more of the relationship, then you need to clarify that you're only there to help the client to resolve his or her own struggles, to provide support as he or she does this, and the relationship is bounded by the counselor's office.

If you find yourself slipping over your client's boundaries, trying to express or show your own affection, or trying to take control of the client's situation, then you need to bring this to the attention of your supervisor, or experienced mentor, and explore how you can better respect the client's boundaries and reign yourself in. You need to be aware of your own feelings and impulses and remind yourself you have an ethical responsibility to stay within the context of a helpful counseling relationship.

YOUR OWN COMFORT WITH FEELINGS

When you use the rapport building and active listening skills with clients, some of what they disclose to you will be the problems they have within their status quo. In turn, if you help to explore the consequences of these problems, feelings will be triggered by the client's expanded awareness of the costs. You must be able to handle these feelings and to accept some level of negative emotions as a normal outcome of expanded awareness of the problems and their implications. You need to be able to fully join your client in discovery of the feelings that lie within his or her Reality Trough.

When we train counselors to use these skills, some trainees say, "I feel uncomfortable when my clients get into their deeper feelings. I don't know what to do when they feel extremely sad, angry, hurt, or desperate. Do I really have to deal with such feelings in this approach?" This is a typical response from people who early in life learned to shut the door on feelings and to act as if their own feelings didn't exist.

However, we think it's better for the client to confront those feelings. This allows the emotions to surface as the client realizes the need to take action. This helps the client get to the point of saying, "This sucks. Let's do something about this. What can I do?"

This isn't psychotherapy. We aren't asking you to fix "broken" people. But Insight Counseling is about the client making a change. To be motivated to make a change, the client benefits when all the costs of not changing are known. Your client will get ready for change when he or she goes through the Reality Trough.

Bringing the implications of the status quo into full awareness will surface negative emotions along with the realization the costs are higher than the person was admitting to him or herself. Assist the surfacing of these client feelings and the client's motivation to change will rise.

Notice your own discomfort with your clients' expressions of intense feelings and see this difficulty as your problem, one you need to solve if you intend to continue counseling others. Talk with your supervisor or more experienced mentor about the discomfort you have. Try to unearth where that discomfort comes from. From some earlier learnings, you likely concluded that exploring intense feelings is overwhelming or leads to trouble in some way. You will have to challenge that belief if you want to be effective.

PERSONAL USE OF LISTENING SKILLS

I've identified effective interpersonal skills for listening to achieve full understanding and I've emphasized you should use them particularly during the engagement step of the counseling process and in step three while you get your client's S.P.I.C.E[3]:

- invitations, and explained invitations,

- paraphrasing,

- inference checking,

- feelings checking,

- identification,

- exploratory questions including assumptive, multiple choice, "best of all possible worlds", and explained questions,

and

- matching – subconscious paraphrasing showing the client you really want to understand what it means to be him or her.

I hope you choose to frequently use these skills in your work, as active listening will enrich your counseling interactions with clients. Use these skills to get clients talking and help your clients to find the reasons and motivation to change.

However, these skills will also enrich your personal life if you use them more often in your own relationships. Your spouse, your children, your friends, and co-workers will appreciate you when you give the gift of listening to their needs to achieve full understanding. Using these skills will mean your significant others will open up with you and disclose more about themselves. When you use these skills, the other person feels he or she can trust you.

Use the skills wherever you have an opportunity to listen to others. This will build your proficiency with the skills and make such use much more natural when you engage in your counseling activities. If you get so comfortable with the skills you don't have to think about them, you become unconsciously competent. This frees you up to pay more attention to your client than to your own responses.

It's a safe assumption you already know how to use these skills. However, most people use them all too seldom. I urge you to deliberately use these skills when counseling, and I also urge you to increase your use of these skills with those you love and care about.

Using active listening skills is significantly better for your own well being, the well being of your clients, and the well being of your family and friends. Active listening is better than using the behaviors known to get in the way of achieving rapport and understanding.

BEHAVIORS THAT INTERFERE

Getting the client's S.P.I.C.E[3] is a process of using particular communication skills to help your client to open up and share all elements of his or her story. Be as skilled as you can be at using the active listening skills and use them in the right balance to facilitate empathy and to help your client trust you.

However, just as you want to develop increased use of the active listening skills, you need to curb use of those behaviors that interfere with open communication. There are certain behaviors that get in the way of listening for understanding, and you have to guard yourself from using them.

- **Giving Advice** – offering a possible solution in response to something the client has just said.

- **Listening For Just The Facts** – focusing so much on the facts that the position, ideas, or emotions the facts are intended to convey are missed.

- **Not Taking Notes** – relying on memory, which gets harder to do when the story gets more complex, and consequently important parts of the story are forgotten.

- **Distractions** – putting up with or causing distractions like the clicking of a pen, talking with someone else while the speaker is talking, or doing something else while listening

- **Emotional Distractions** – having specific feelings in response to something the speaker says that trigger your own thoughts about prior situations, thereby taking your attention away from what is being communicated.

- **Preconceptions** – not listening to what the client says because of some preconceived idea (*i.e. hearing something that makes you think he or she is just like other clients*).

- **Embarrassment** – missing something your client said and being too embarrassed to ask him or her to repeat it, or being too intimidated to give back your interpretation out of fear you are wrong.

- **Interruptions** – cutting off or otherwise interrupting the client because you think you have something more important to say or ask.

- **Premature Directive Questions** – cutting off the flow of the client's story by asking a pointed or direct question that changes the subject and directs the client to attend to what you think is important, before the client has had a chance to tell you what he or she thinks is most important.

- **Criticizing** – privately thinking about or publicly commenting on negative aspects of the client or what he or she is telling you instead of learning his or her full meaning.

- **Faking Attention or Rehearsing** – thinking of something other than what the client is saying, or mentally preparing what to say next, or thinking about the next question.

- **Prejudging** – forming a negative opinion about the client, adopting a negative attitude, and tuning the speaker out (*for example, by deciding the client probably won't change much*).

Discipline yourself to avoid these behaviors. They just get in the way of open conversations. Notice what happens inside you when others do these things to you as you tell your own stories.

GIVING ADVICE

Giving advice headed my list of behaviors that will get in the way and I want to give more attention to how this can interfere. Advice giving is quite counter productive, even destructive, to the "GET STOKED & ACT" counseling approach.

If you give advice to your client, you're doing several things at once:

- assuming you know enough to suggest the right solution for your client, but your advice may not be appropriate because you might not really understand the client's needs, and your client may not yet know enough about his or her S.P.I.C.E[3] to truly welcome your suggestion,

- assuming you know better than the client what he or she should do,

- taking responsibility for the client's problem away from the client,

- assuming your client can't solve his or her problem, thereby sending a self-esteem diminishing message to your client,

- stimulating client resistance as he or she recognizes your advice is not appropriate for the client's S.P.I.C.E[3], or when you offer your advice before the client is ready for change,

- undermining the learning the client could do about how to solve his or her problems on his or her own,

- turning a cooperative relationship built on empathy and trust into an adversarial relationship built on suspicion, distrust, and the need for the client to protect him or her self from you,

and

- putting the client's burden on yourself, making yourself feel emotionally heavier as you listen to your client's stories.

None of these results lead to the client finding a creative and effective solution to his or her problem(s), and subvert the second goal of having the client learn to be a more effective problem-solver for work on future problems. In addition, you do yourself harm by taking over ownership of the problem. Stop yourself from giving advice.

LOOK AFTER YOURSELF

Counselors place themselves in danger by spending a significant chunk of their time listening to others who struggle. This process can too easily pull one down, especially when you're learning to be a counselor, or when you're bumping up against persistent client resistance to change. If you continuously listen to negative talk, your own perceptions of your world may take on the color of grey.

If you intend to devote significant time to the role of counselor, you need to develop some strategies for taking care of yourself as you do.

FIND EFFECTIVE WAYS TO RELAX AND CALM YOURSELF

I recommend you build time into your day for either or both of physical activity and meditation. Being active will burn off any frustration energy that builds up as you listen to your clients and will ultimately relax your body. Mediation will quiet an overactive mind and thereby relax your body. Both will separate you from your client's struggles. Both will also allow your own creative juices to flow and you may find suggestions emerging from your subconscious mind for how you could potentially be more helpful to your clients.

BE MORE RESISTANT THAN YOUR CLIENTS

One way to take care of you is to stop pushing for change. Find your own patience, and learn to set aside your own feelings of urgency to fix your clients. Look for reasons why your client shouldn't change just yet. Look for the positives in your client's personal status quo, reinforce these both in your own mind and for your client. Truly accept that what the client has achieved so far is remarkable and worthy of respect.

Back off to go slow and you might paradoxically discover change will happen faster. Work only to learn the client's S.P.I.C.E^3, taking your client through his or her Reality Trough so the client moves at his or her own pace to a readiness for change. Resist pushing for change as you help your client shift to readiness. It will be much easier for you to be the helper.

FIND YOUR OWN SOURCE OF COUNSELING OR MENTORSHIP

Don't keep all of the feelings your clients trigger in you to yourself. Find your own confidant, someone with more experience, someone you can trust, someone with which you can express any concerns you have about your counseling, or your relationships with your clients. Open up. Express those feelings and explore any thoughts you have about the problems you're having being as helpful as you would like. Explore your own S.P.I.C.E^3.

Schedule regular sessions with a mentor and use the opportunity to review what you've been doing with your clients. Choose a mentor that listens effectively and actively, reflecting back what he or she hears and sees as you talk. Take this opportunity to learn more about yourself. If you're carrying any tensions, frustrations, feelings that you are burdened by your clients stories, then express these feelings to release their hold on you.

PAY ATTENTION TO YOUR OWN DEVELOPMENT OF THESE SKILLS

Lastly, you can take better care of yourself as a counselor by constantly reviewing how you're applying the counseling skills. Review your work with your clients and examine what you've done well, where you've bumped up against roadblocks, and what you can learn from this review. Reinforce your own personal development by noticing it, congratulating yourself for it, and feeling some pride in your accomplishments. Look at areas needing improvement with some excitement knowing you can apply the same discipline to find new ways to improve. Feel confidence in your ability to continuously learn.

THE "GET STOKED & ACT" AGENDA

Use "GET STOKED & ACT" as your own personal agenda during your counseling sessions. When you follow an organized counseling sequence and use specific techniques to successfully complete each step in the sequence, counseling effectiveness increases. With this agenda, you can confidently offer assistance to your clients, whether or not they are resistant, totally discouraged, confused, or in pain. In this way, you become an effective change agent.

THE FIRST PART: GET

	STEP	ACTIVITY
G	Greet.	Show sincere interest in the client and begin a conversation.
E	Engage.	Continue the conversation building an open relationship.
T	Take Time To Get the Client's S.P.I.C.E³.	Get the client's S.P.I.C.E³ by actively listening to the client such that he or she does most of the talking while you clarify for understanding (*reaching for deeper insight*).
	The Shift	*Make a mental shift toward inviting your client to engage in problem-solving.*

195

In the first part of this approach, you're getting information from your client and helping him or her to organize it into a workable problem definition. You must greet and engage your client in a conversation that gets quite personal, encouraging the client to open up and share information with you about his or her struggles. You need to show empathy, respect and compassion.

Reach for full understanding as this delivers new insights to your clients. This helps your client to gain new insights about his or her S.P.I.C.E^3, helps your client get ready for change, and both of you get to know just exactly what the problem is that needs to be solved. Establish rapport with your client and build his or her trust in you as someone who can help to solve the current problem(s) and as someone from whom he or she can learn how to be more self-sufficient.

THE SECOND PART: STOKED

	STEP	ACTIVITY
S	Summarize The Problem.	Summarize what you've learned about the client's S.P.I.C.E^3, explaining that this is the problem definition.
T	Teach Creative Problem-Solving Steps.	Present the problem-solving steps you're going to help your client to navigate.
O	Option Search (Generate Many Solutions)	Engage in brainstorming by using techniques that stimulate creativity.
K	Know Each Idea	Clarify, elaborate, expand and merge ideas into more complete solution possibilities.
E	Evaluate Each Solution Option	Consider the pros and cons of each idea and measure each option against the client's decision criteria.
D	Decide (Make The Selection)	Get your client to choose the optimum solution or set of solutions.

In the second part, you teach your client how to engage effectively in creative problem-solving. You explain the steps you're going to follow to find an optimum solution to the problem the two of you have identified. You emphasize the importance of following a structured process to get creative to find solutions to tough problems. Then you work together to engage in creative thinking to randomly generate and enhance solution possibilities.

After you have generated many solution possibilities, teach your client to make a mental shift and switch to critical, judgmental, evaluative, and selective thinking to decide which solution(s) will work best. From there, your client identifies an optimum solution and chooses the change he or she wants to make.

THE THIRD PART: ACT

A	Action Plan	Help your client sort out when and where he or she will implement the solution, how he or she will do so, what resources he or she will use, how your client will keep him or her self on track, and why each action is being done.
C	Change	Get your client to put the solution(s) into effect according to the plan. If possible, watch the client as he or she implements the solution and intervene if the plan is breaking down.
T	Tally The Results – Assess How Well The Client Has Done	Some time after the client has implemented his or her solution(s), sit down together and assess how well the solution(s) worked; and talk about how the client feels about the process of change he or she went through while working with you.

Help your client to ACT. In the third part, help your client to develop an action plan for implementing the chosen solution(s). Make sure your client has the best chance of succeeding when he or she executes the solution by knowing exactly who will do what, when, where, how, with what resources, and why. Then after the client has implemented the solution, help your client to tally the results to determine if he or she achieved the desired goal by the deadline he or she set.

The third part also includes an assessment of how effective your counseling has been for both you and the client. You want to assess your own performance so you learn from each counseling interaction what you need to change to be more effective with future clients.

* * *

Using this insight-oriented problem-solving process, you may be surprised by the solutions that emerge and the results your client's realize. Your clients will more likely achieve synergy – a result that is significantly better than your client might have believed possible before tackling the problem.

When you think it's too complex for a given problem or a given client, use the **SIMPLIFICATION OPTIONS**. I've presented ways you can still achieve the "STOKED & ACT" portions of this approach by conversationally guiding the client's behavior to the appropriate steps in creative problem-solving.

Discipline yourself to work through this sequence on a regular, everyday basis and you'll get substantially faster at working this way. Your ability to listen effectively to arrive at a clearly understood definition of your client's problem(s) will grow with practice and repetition.

You'll have more fun with your clients as you engage in the creative thinking process. Your clients will find and choose new solutions that empower them to take better control over their own lives.

The quality of your results as a counselor will rise and your success will be noticeable. In addition, this skill set will move from conscious competence, where you have to deliberately think about what you're doing, to unconscious competence, where it just happens subconsciously. When you repeatedly follow this approach, it slowly becomes something you hardly have to think about.

"GET STOKED & ACT"

APPENDICES

APPENDIX 1: "GET STOKED & ACT"

	STEP
G	Greet
E	Engage
T	Take Time To Get The Client's S.P.I.C.E^3
	The Shift
S	Summarize The Problem (The Client's S.P.I.C.E^3)
T	Teach The Problem-Solving steps.
O	Option Search (Generate Solution Possibilities)
K	Know Each Idea (Elaborate, Expand And Clarify)
E	Evaluate Each Solution Option
D	Decide (Get The Client To Make A Selection)

A	Action Plan
C	Change
T	Tally The Results – Assess How Well The Client Has Done, And Assess How Well You've Done As a Counselor

APPENDIX 2: THE S.P.I.C.E³ ELEMENTS

Situation	The client's current situation; what he or she experiences; where the client experiences what he or she has to deal with; who else might be involved; what resources the client has available to use now; how he or she copes or manages the current situation; why the client has these experiences.
Problems	The symptoms, difficulties, real problems, opportunities, and challenges the client has when doing what he or she does; and what wishes he or she has to do it better.
Implications	What these problems cost the client, both tangibly and intangibly; and what feelings the client has about these costs, including feelings about lost opportunities.
Constraints	Why the client hasn't fixed these problems or concerns before now; and what has blocked him or her from taking appropriate action.
E³xpectations, excitement, and eagerness	What the client would minimally expect to gain; what results would really excite the client (*reduced costs, improved performance, new opportunities, new results and benefits*); and how eager the client is to get the problem solved.

APPENDIX 3: THE PROBLEM DEFINITION

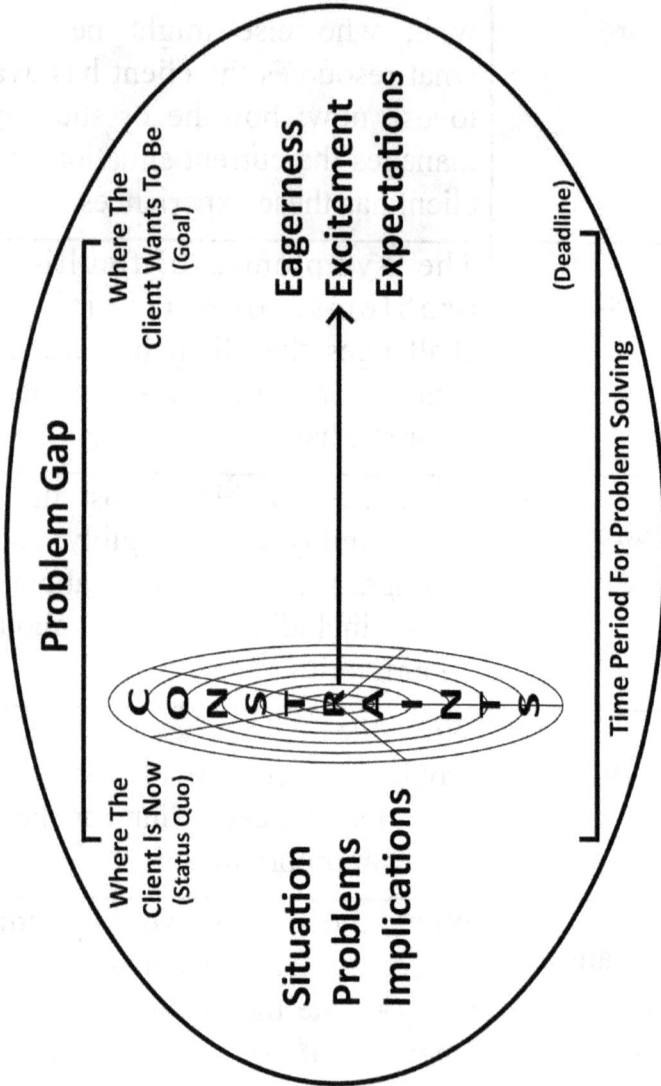

Problem Gap

Where The Client Wants To Be (Goal)

Where The Client Is Now (Status Quo)

Eagerness
Excitement
Expectations

Situation
Problems
Implications

CONSTRAINTS

Time Period For Problem Solving

(Deadline)

APPENDIX 4: THE S.P.I.C.E³ SHEET

Client: _____ Tel. No. _____

SITUATION

_____

_____

_____

_____

PROBLEMS

_____

_____

_____

_____

IMPLICATIONS/COSTS

_____

_____

_____

_____

CONSTRAINTS

_____

_____

_____

EXPECTATIONS, EXCITING BENEFITS, EAGERNESS

_____

_____

_____

APPENDIX 5: THE PROBLEM-SOLVING STEPS (TASKS AND SKILLS)

Step	Task
Feel The Need	Feel the gap between where you are and where you want to be. Recognize at some level, even just subconsciously, that you feel a gap.
Define The Problem (S.P.I.C.E³)	Sort through your S.P.I.C.E³ – situation, problem, implications, constraints, expectations, excitements, and eagerness; then specify the criteria a solution must satisfy to be a viable solution (available resources constraints to overcome, deadline and desired E^3 outcomes).
Generate Solution Possibilities	Engage in uncensored, creative thinking and generate as many solutions ideas as you can in a defined time period.
Elaborate and Clarify	Expand on ideas, merge ideas together to make them even better, and clarify the full meaning of the expanded ideas.
Evaluate	Evaluate each idea, positives first then limitations, and determine whether or not the idea meets your decision criteria.
Decide	Decide which solution or set of solutions will give you the best possible results.
Action Plan	Determine when you will do what, where, when, how, with what resources, and why.
Implement	Act on your decision by implementing your solution according to your plan.
Assess	Determine if the solution produced your desired results and review how well you followed the problem-solving model.

Step	Skills
Feel The Need	Notice Any Feelings Or Thoughts You Have That Something Could Be Better Than It Is
Define The Problem (S.P.I.C.E[3])	Write Out Your S.P.I.C.E[3] • Situation. • Problems (symptoms, frustrations, difficulties, opportunities). • Implications or costs of the problems. • Constraints and roadblocks. • Minimal expectations, highly desired results, deadlines.
Generate Solution Possibilities	Brainstorm Many Solution Possibilities • Set a definite time period. • Think of and say out loud as many ideas as you can. • Think of unusual, far-out, imaginative, even absurd ideas. • No evaluation. • Record all ideas. • Cheer yourself on for coming up with many ideas.
Elaborate and Clarify	Complete An Idea/Elaboration/Clarification Sheet For All Ideas • Make ideas bigger. • Merge ideas. • Guess at all possible meanings.

Evaluate	Look At Positive Attributes Of Each Idea First Then Assess Weaknesses • Do Pro/Con or Advantage/Disadvantage lists. • Measure each idea against your decision criteria.
Decide	Pick A Set of Solutions That Could Work Together To Produce The Best Results
Action Plan	Specify When You Will Do What, Where, When, How, With What Resources, And Why. • Record The Plan.
Implement	Act On Your Decision By Implementing Your Solution According To Your Plan. • Where possible, do so in a trial situation first.
Assess	Determine How Well You Did • Measure results. • Review your problem-solving behavior looking for strengths and weaknesses.

APPENDIX 6: BRAINSTORMING

1. Set a definite time period for solution generation and generate ideas throughout (Stick to that time limit).

2. Use a time period for solution generation that parallels the significance and difficulty of the problem.

3. Think of and say out loud as many options as you can in the time allowed.

4. Think of unusual, far out, imaginative, even absurd ideas.

5. Suspend all censorship – there should be no evaluation or criticism of any option during this period.

6. Record all options as they are said out loud, without censorship or modification in the act of recording each idea.

7. Record even those options that the recorder might think have been expressed already.

and

8. Cheer yourself on and make encouraging comments about the growing number of options – not the quality of the ideas themselves.

Brainstorming Rules

> **Set A Time Limit, Stick To It**
> **As Many Ideas As Possible**
> **Weird and Far-out Ideas**
> **No Evaluation**
> **Record All Ideas**
> **Encourage Quantity**

APPENDIX 7: IDEAS, ELABORATION AND CLARIFICATION

IDEA	ELABORATION (Expand Each Idea. Flesh It Out)	CLARIFICATION (Understand The Full Idea)

ACKNOWLEDGEMENTS

I had the opportunity to teach counseling skills workshops to a variety of adults who worked in some sort of counseling or helping role. I thank them for their enthusiastic participation in counseling role-plays putting my ideas to the test. Some of these workshops were offered through the University of Alberta, Department of Continuing Education, while others were conducted during the training and consultation services I provided for a great number of health, education, and social service workers under the auspices of the Edmonton Board of Health. I thank both of these organizations for giving me an opportunity to do such work.

I wish to thank Bernie Spak for his contributions as we developed the concept of S.P.I.C.E^3 when building the consultative and problem-solving sales model called the SMART selling system. S.P.I.C.E^3 became the acronym and framework for a full and complete problem definition.

I wish to thank my counseling instructors at the University of Alberta, Faculty of Education, Department of Educational Psychology and those colleagues that shared their thinking about counseling, permitted me to observe their work with clients, and watched me work with my own and provided feedback.

I thank those people who trusted me as their counseling psychologist and shared their stories and problems with me, accepting my many interventions to help them achieve their desired changes.

I thank Ray Rasmussen for the ideas and concepts he shared with me when he was teaching problem-solving to his Business Administration students in undergraduate and Master's level programs at the University of Alberta. Ray also provided guidance on the self publishing process that facilitated getting this document out of my word processor and into printed book format through CreateSpace and the digital format for Kindle. Katherine Caine read a draft of the manuscript and offered her suggestions and edits to make this much more readable.

I thank them all for their contributions. However I take full ownership of any errors, omissions, or inadequacies.

ABOUT THE AUTHOR

GARY R. FORD, MBA, PHD

At the University of Alberta, Gary achieved undergraduate and master's degrees in business administration plus a PhD in Educational Psychology. Following his education, Gary worked as a lecturer in the business program at the University of Alberta, then subsequently worked at the Edmonton Board of Health as a registered psychologist doing counseling with individuals, couples, and families, as well as organizational development work with health, social service, legal and educational institutions. He left the Board of Health to then work as a Counseling Psychologist in private practice. Through this work he developed his listening skills and expanded his understanding of change processes and systems theory.

Seeking practical experience in effective development of his own organization, he then made a radical career choice and operated a retail and corporate sales organization for 20 years, after which he entered his first retirement. Unable to sit still for long, he then worked as a Dean of Business with a start-up Canadian university for five years. Following the death of his spouse of 43 years, he retired again; and used his time to write and develop training materials on sales, creative problem-solving, and counseling.

Gary is currently spending his time engaged in writing and amateur photography. You can see his work at www.garyrford.ca.

INSIGHT
PUBLISHERS

**Box 2 Site 3 RR #1 South
Thorsby, Alberta, Canada
T0C 2P0
www.garyrford.ca/insight**

Other Insight Books Published By This Author

Insight Sales: (Retail)

Insight Sales (Corporate)

Insight Sales (Corporate and Retail)

A Quick Guide To Insight Sales

Insight Solutions: Creative Problem-Solving

Other Published Books

intimate moments: A Haibun Collection

www.ingramcontent.com/pod-product-compliance
Lightning Source LLC
Chambersburg PA
CBHW050114280326
41933CB00010B/1099